teach®
yourself

**things to do
as a family**
debbie musselwhite

Launched in 1938, the **teach yourself** series grew rapidly in response to the world's wartime needs. Loved and trusted by over 50 million readers, the series has continued to respond to society's changing interests and passions and now, 70 years on, includes over 500 titles, from Arabic and Beekeeping to Yoga and Zulu. What would you like to learn?

be where you want to be with **teach yourself**

Orders: please contact Bookpoint Ltd, 130 Milton Park, Abingdon, Oxon, OX14 4SB. Telephone: +44 (0) 1235 827720. Fax: +44 (0) 1235 400454. Lines are open 09.00–17.00, Monday to Saturday, with a 24-hour message answering service. Details about our titles and how to order are available at www.teachyourself.co.uk

Long renowned as the authoritative source for self-guided learning – with more than 50 million copies sold worldwide – the **teach yourself** series includes over 500 titles in the fields of languages, crafts, hobbies, business, computing and education.

British Library Cataloguing in Publication Data: a catalogue record for this title is available from the British Library.

First published in UK 2008 by Hodder Education, part of Hachette Livre UK, 338 Euston Road, London, NW1 3BH.

This edition published 2008.

The **teach yourself** name is a registered trade mark of Hodder Headline.

Copyright © 2008 Debbie Musselwhite

Typeset by Transet Limited, Coventry.
Printed in Great Britain for Hodder Education, an Hachette Livre UK Company, 338 Euston Road, London, NW1 3BH, by Cox & Wyman Ltd, Reading, Berkshire.

The publisher has used its best endeavours to ensure that the URLs for external websites referred to in this book are correct and active at the time of going to press. However, the publisher and the author have no responsibility for the websites and can make no guarantee that a site will remain live or that the content will remain relevant, decent or appropriate.

Hachette Livre UK's policy is to use papers that are natural, renewable and recyclable products and made from wood grown in sustainable forests. The logging and manufacturing processes are expected to conform to the environmental regulations of the country of origin.

Impression number   10 9 8 7 6 5 4 3 2 1
Year   2012 2011 2010 2009 2008

contents

acknowledgements

With thanks to **www.gameskidsplay.net** for information about childhood games.

Sandcastle photograph © Manuel Abadia (p.29); Paper plane by Paul Doherty, from Exploratorium Magazine 'Exploring Paper', 23:2, spring 1999, adapted with permission © Exploratorium **www.exploratorium.edu** (p.54); Chinese Lion Puppet,text and photographs reproduced by kind permission of **www.activityvillage.co.uk** (pp.59-60); Fortune cookies recipe adapted from **www.chiff.com**, Chiff Chef Recipe File, submitted by Nancy W. (p.60); Candle holder adapted from **www.activityvillage.co.uk** (p.71); Kheer recipe from **www.activityvillage.co.uk** (p.72); Quick pumpkin pie recipe adapted from **www.activityvillage.co.uk** (pp.73-4); Rollerblading text adapted from **www.tellmehowto.net** (pp.126-7); Rules for Jacks copyright of Masters Traditional Games, an internet shop selling quality traditional games, pub games and unusual games. To find out more, visit **www.mastersgames.com** (p.131); Juggling text and illustrations adapted from **www.pandas.currantbun.com/Juggling** (pp.142-3); Card tricks adapted from **www.card-trick.com** (pp.144-5); Chess rules content partly adapted from **www.geocities.com/CapeCanaveral/Lab/8354** (pp.150-1); Pop up card adapted from **www.enchantedlearning.com** (p.158); Feather game from **www.activityvillage.co.uk** (pp.175-6); Musical instrument instructions reproduced by kind permission of **www.traditionalmusic.co.uk** (pp.166-170); Musical bottles from **lhsweb@berkeley.edu** (p.171-2); Hunt the Thimble from **www.activityvillage.co.uk** (p.181).

introduction

This book is about having fun with your children – about engaging them in good, old-fashioned activities guaranteed to lure them away from the TV, computer and all the other screen distractions that keep them glued to the sofa. From snap to gin rummy, tiddlywinks to chess, marbles to charades, all the old favourite games are here, plus some less familiar ones. Spur your children into action with outdoor pursuits like rounders and French cricket. Make the most of rainy days with a wealth of indoor interests to keep them occupied and interested. Teach your child how to knit, make musical instruments (ear plugs not supplied!), cultivate flowers and vegetables, make coconut ice – the list is endless. Also included are longer projects you can involve your children in during the holidays.

Something for every occasion

Whether you are at home with the kids or outside, travelling or on holiday, you'll find something to interest your child for every occasion and situation, including card games, puzzles, classic board games and easy crafts. While the activities are aimed at five to 12 year olds, you'd be surprised how much older children will enjoy taking part in them – even superior, moody teenagers.

And the best thing about all these activities is that they cost very little money and take little effort to do. Instead of spending hours stuck in a traffic jam en route to yet another theme park, you and your children could be playing rounders in the local park, fossil hunting on the beach or building a bird table in the garden. Chances are you're already doing some of these anyway, but it's always worth having a few surprises up your sleeve when the kids are stuck indoors on a rainy day, or squabbling on an interminable car journey.

Back to basics

Before the advent of TV, families had to make their own entertainment – hence the huge popularity of card games, puzzles, indoor pursuits, conjuring, amateur theatricals, billiards, chess, draughts... Going back even further to Victorian times, 'manly' games and exercise were all the rage – schoolboys played a huge range of rough, boisterous games such as Battle for the Banner and Baste the Bear.

We've rounded up the best activities from the past, and in reviving these games and pastimes with your children you'll be creating lasting childhood memories. While your children may not remember watching the latest Disney film with you, what they will hold dear will be the things you did together.

> **Teach yourself Things to do as a family** is packed with activities you and your children can share.

Benefits for the whole family

By engaging your children in activities – whether it's teaching them how to play cards or making something – you'll be equipping them with vital skills which will stand them in good stead when they're older. You'll be helping them to:

- boost their confidence and self-esteem – mastering a new game or making something gives children a huge sense of achievement and pride in their endeavour
- understand the importance of interacting with others and playing by the rules
- improve their concentration
- be patient and persistent and not give in at the first setback
- accept defeat gracefully
- take responsibility for decisions taken, even if it's the wrong one

- learn useful skills such as counting, memorization and logical reasoning.

In turn your reward will be:

- happier, more engaged children
- a closer sense of family.

Doing things with your children strengthens the bond between you, creating a more harmonious atmosphere. It builds relationships, develops shared interests and gives you the chance to play too. It brings you and your child to the same level, with shared goals. It relaxes you because it involves you. Even making a daisy chain together will give you both a sense of achievement. And in an age when child safety is of paramount importance, you can relax, knowing that your children are engaged in safe, wholesome pursuits.

Pick your activity

Pick and choose an activity to suit you and your children – nothing should be a chore or hard work. If it is, then choose something else. The key word is fun! Nowadays, when time is at a premium, bear in mind that it's the quality of the time you spend with your children, not the quantity. It is far better to get the whole family to join in and enjoy half an hour of cards, rather than some enforced activity which you all find dull and boring.

Alternatively, you could set aside a special family activities evening, for example, every Friday, so children can stay up a little later. If you don't have a big family, or you're a single parent, invite friends and their children over. However you want to arrange it, you'll be creating your own family tradition which your children will remember with pleasure in the years to come.

Plan a menu of activities to suit younger and older children, mixing silly, noisy games with quieter, more reflective activities so they're not totally hyped up for bedtime. Here are some ideas to get you started though obviously you can make up your own selection.

Sample menu for a family evening				
Activity	Type	Age range	No of players	Rating
Cheat	Card game	5 upwards	2 upwards	Easy, relying on ability to cheat with a straight face
Up Jenkins	Table game	5 upwards	4 upwards	Easy. Expect lots of shrieking!
Snap	Classic card game	5 upwards	2 upwards	Very easy
Picture con-sequences	Drawing game	4 upwards	2 upwards	Easy and produces lots of laughs
Dominoes	Played with tiles	5 upwards	2 upwards	Easy
Fanning the kipper	Relay team game	5 upwards	4 upwards	Very easy
Charades	Word game	5 upwards	2 upwards	Easy to hard, depending on words chosen

Of course all these activities can be enjoyed at any time, and after school is a good time for arts and crafts and cookery. Youngsters can also join in more challenging card games such as Crazyfights or Newmarket if you play in teams.

Energy boosters

Outdoor games are a brilliant way to get children off the sofa and on the move. There are all sorts of games you can play outside – there are hundreds of derivatives of the game of tag, for example. Some of the best games of all are the ones you can play outside in wide open spaces like softball, frisbee, touch football, volleyball, badminton and croquet.

What you'll need

While the majority of activities mentioned in this book require little more than paper and pens, it's worth collecting a few items to have ready when boredom strikes. These could include:

- playing cards
- board games
- scrap paper and pencils
- egg timer
- sports equipment – football, tennis balls, racquets, shuttlecocks, Frisbee
- recycled materials for crafts such as: empty egg boxes and cereal packets, pipe cleaners, shoeboxes, string, picture postcards, thin card, balsa wood, fabric scraps, old magazines, buttons, gold and silver paper, adhesive, scissors, empty matchboxes, paints and colouring pencils (see Chapter 09 for a fuller list).

These are just some ideas to get you started and over the following chapters you'll find many more suggestions to make the most of your time with your children.

To end on a note of caution, make sure you always supervise your children if they're engaged in any activity which could involve an accident, indoors or outdoors. Pay particular attention if they're using craft knives or cooking. You will also be instilling a sense of safety in them, which is another vital lesson.

Note: Throughout the book we tend to refer to 'children' in the plural. This is just for convenience, so don't feel you've been left out if you have just one child. Many of the activities mentioned can be played by two people anyway.

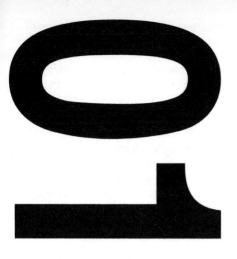

01

on the move: travelling with children

In this chapter you will learn:
- how to prepare for a long journey
- ways to keep the kids entertained on long journeys, including word puzzles, games and songs
- tips for travelling by car, train and plane
- how to cope with airport delays.

Whatever sort of family holiday you have planned – short break or long haul – it's bound to involve a degree of travelling, whether you're going by car, plane, train or coach. In an ideal world children would be model travellers, never squabbling, complaining or fidgeting. However, in reality they can get horribly bored and fed up on long journeys and your dream of a happy family holiday can rapidly dissolve into a nightmare of sulky, squabbling kids and exasperated, stressed-out parents.

However, you'll be glad to hear it doesn't have to be that way. Keep your kids occupied with plenty of games, puzzles and other distractions and they won't have time to grumble, plus they'll be exercising their brains in the bargain. Bear in mind too that while you see the journey as a means to an end, for children the journey in itself can be incredibly exciting, full of fascinating sights and sounds, so harness this interest and make the most of it.

Planning your journey

The secret to harmonious travel with children lies in planning ahead. Assume that at some stage of the journey your children are going to get restless, especially if you've got a lot of miles to cover, so take this into account when you're planning your route. If you're going by car or coach, show them where you'll be going on the map – the more they feel involved in the journey, the less likely they are to grumble about the length of it once you get going. Give each child a list of the towns you'll be going through, so they can tick them off as you pass them.

If you're driving, you could also ask your children to pick out interesting places they'd like to visit en route. This might mean extra travelling time, but your reward will be children excitedly looking forward to a break at a place they've chosen themselves.

Make a list in advance of family games you can play on the journey. Include some new ones (with brief instructions) as well as family favourites to make it more interesting. Obviously you need to choose games to suit the way you're travelling – playing noisy word games on a plane won't exactly endear you or your children to the other passengers – but most of the activities we've included can be played anywhere, and serve as useful distractions if you're stuck in a traffic jam or if your flight's been delayed.

If you're driving, stick the list on the dashboard so you can refer to it the instant you hear the dreaded 'Are we there yet?'. If you're flying or going by train, pop the list in your bag.

It's also a good idea to get your children to take their own activity bags packed with their favourite things such as personal stereos, MP3 players, books, story tapes – anything which will help entertain them on the journey. (You could also add your games list.) Encourage them to pack their own bag so they can't blame you for anything left behind!

Don't leave home without...

Whatever sort of journey you have planned, these essential travel items will help keep children entertained and arguments to a minimum:

- spare batteries for hand-held consoles
- magnetic travel games such as Snakes and Ladders, Solitaire, Noughts and Crosses, Draughts and Chess
- playing cards – as well as a traditional pack, include favourite card games such as Snap and Happy Families
- paper, pencils and felt-tips
- story tapes
- Frisbee and/or soft ball
- comics, magazines and books (including this one!)

Making memories

Encouraging your children to keep a record of their holiday will keep them busy and involved in the journey. They'll also enjoy looking at mementoes of their trip when they return home, sharing them with their friends or the rest of their class. Here are some ideas you could suggest to your children:

- **Collecting souvenirs** Throughout the journey your children could collect things that remind them of where they've been, such as shells and pebbles from beaches, postcards from different towns, stamps/flags from different countries, bumper stickers, snowglobes and so on.

- **Keeping a holiday diary** Encourage your children to keep a daily diary of what they've done. They could stick in postcards, tickets, programmes, receipts, brochures etc.

- **Taking photos** This is one of the best ways of preserving holiday memories. Give each child a disposable camera so you don't have to worry if it gets lost. Get the photos printed while you're still away so they can put them into a scrapbook, with dates and brief descriptions about each photo.

Brainteasers for long journeys

These fun and challenging games will keep the whole family occupied on the journey. They can all be played on trains, coaches, planes and in the car.

Counting crows

A counting game which also tests your children's observational skills. Players have to count a particular number of animals or objects on their side of the road, for example, ten cows, eight tractors or 15 road signs – anything you like. To make it more challenging, particular objects can send scores back to zero, such as a black dog in town, or a service station on the motorway. The winner is the person who reaches the highest number once you've reached your destination.

Animal, vegetable or mineral

One player thinks of something that can be classified as animal, vegetable or mineral and tells the other players which category it falls into. The other players take it in turns to ask up to 20 questions to try to find out what the object is. They can only ask questions that can be answered with a 'yes' or 'no'. For instance, if the word is 'elephant', which is an animal, the game might go like this:

'Is it furry?'
'No.'
'Does it eat meat?'
'No.'
'Is it big?'
'Yes.'
'Does it live in hot countries?'
'Yes.'
'Does it live on land?'
'Yes.'
'Is it very strong?'
'Yes.'
'Is it an elephant?'
'Yes!'

The game continues in this vein until the players have used up 20 questions. If someone guesses the word – i.e. 'elephant' in this case – it's their turn. If no one guesses the word, the same player chooses another word.

Connections

The first player says the name of an object, for example 'carrot'. The next player has to say a word related to this word, for example, 'rabbit', the connection being that rabbits eat carrots. The player after that has to come up with a word related to 'rabbit', for example, 'Easter' (the connection being the Easter bunny), and so the game continues. If you can't think up a connecting word you're out, and the winner is the last person left in the game.

Ghost

The aim is to avoid finishing a word. The first player starts the game by saying a letter. Each player then adds a letter in turn, while thinking up a word that begins with the letters already announced. For example, if the letters in play are THI, a player might have the word THISTLE in mind. If a player adds a letter and makes a word by mistake, a player calls out 'That's a word!' and the player is given a penalty in the form of the letter 'G', the first letter in the word GHOST. The first player to complete the word GHOST is out. If you think that the player before you didn't actually have a word in mind when they said a letter, then you can challenge them. If you are right, they are 'fined' with a letter in the word GHOST. If you are wrong, you are given a letter.

I-spy

The easiest word game ever which can keep kids absorbed for ages. One player chooses an object which everyone can see and announces, 'I spy with my little eye something beginning with 'S' (or any other letter, depending on what the object begins with). The other players then have to guess the word. The first person to guess correctly has the next turn. To make it easier for younger children, you could choose colours, for example, 'I spy with my little eye, something coloured blue.'

Just a minute

You will need a stopwatch for this game, or a watch with a second hand, and someone to act as quizmaster. Agree on how many rounds you have to play. The aim of the game is to talk non-stop about a topic for one minute. However, if you hesitate, repeat any words or deviate from the subject other players can challenge you at any time. If the quizmaster upholds the challenge and agrees that the player is guilty of hesitation, repetition or deviation, the challenger is awarded a point and takes the subject over for the rest of the one minute, unless another challenge is made. If this challenge is upheld by the quizmaster, then that challenger takes over the game. The winner is the person who scores the most points at the end of the game. If younger children are playing, you could make the game easier by reducing the length of time players have to talk to 30 seconds, and sticking to very easy subjects. As younger children can be less fluent, you could also adapt the rules slightly, for instance allowing two hesitations and two repetitions.

Limericks

Making up limericks is huge fun and the sillier the better. You can make up your own or everyone can be given a specific place to write about – somewhere you've been to or are going to on your journey. Here's an example:

There was a young man from Peru
Who one day became a gnu.
In the mud he would wallow
And grass he would swallow
And now he resides in a zoo.

The name game

Beautifully simple but highly addictive. The first player says the name of a famous person, who can be alive or dead. The next player has to come up with the name of a famous person, whose first name begins with the first letter of the previous player's surname. For instance, if it's your turn you could say George Washington. The next player has to say a name beginning with 'W', so might say William Hurt. The next player then has to choose a name beginning with 'H' so could say Howard Hughes, and so on. If you can't think up a name you're out and the other players continue until one winner is left.

Once upon a time

This is a great story-telling game which allows children the chance to give free rein to their imagination and have a good laugh along the way. The rules are very simple: the first player starts telling a story, suddenly breaks off and the next player has to continue with it. The beauty of this game is that it can carry on for as long as you like, can take any shape or form, and suits all age groups. Here's an example:

First player: 'One morning I woke up to find a polar bear in my room. It was very...'

Second player: '... Short and wore a baggy dress which hid the fact that...'

Third player: 'It was actually a monkey in disguise with a...'

And so on, until everyone has had enough or can't carry on because they're laughing too much!

Bananas

There's just one rule in this very easy game: whatever question you're asked, you have to reply with the word 'bananas', which can produce some hilarious results. For instance, if you're asked 'What do you wear to school?' you have to answer, 'Bananas'. If you laugh, however, it's the next player's turn. The player who keeps going the longest without laughing is the winner. You can play this using any word you like, so be prepared for some very silly suggestions!

Shopping list

This is a memory game which will sharpen everyone's wits. The first player begins by saying 'I went to the shop and I bought...' followed by an object beginning with the letter 'A'. The next person repeats the sentence, adding something beginning with 'B'. The game carries on in this way until you reach 'Z', at which point you just start from 'A' again.

For example, you say, 'I went to the shop and I bought an armadillo.' The next player could add, 'I went to the shop and I bought an armadillo and a balloon.' The next player might add, 'I went to the shop and I bought an armadillo, a balloon and a corkscrew.' The next player could say, 'I went to the shop and I bought an armadillo, a balloon, a corkscrew and a dog.' And so on, with each player adding a word beginning with the next letter in the alphabet. If a player forgets the order of the words, they are out, and the winner is the last player left in the game.

Town or out

Very similar to The Name Game, but this time a player names a town or city and the next player has to name a town or city starting with the last letter of the previous word. You're not allowed to repeat any names. For example, the first player might say 'London', and the next player has to say a town beginning with 'N', so could say 'Newmarket'. The next player could say 'Tavistock', the next 'Kidderminster' and so on. Instead of towns or cities, you can name animals, vegetables, flowers, birds or food – anything you like. If a player can't think of a name then they are out.

'Yes' 'no' game

A very easy, silly game where you have to avoid saying 'yes' or 'no'. The player fires questions at the second player, trying as hard as possible to trick them into saying 'yes' or 'no'. For example, if the questioner asks you, 'Do you like chocolate?' you have to reply 'I do not like chocolate'. The questioner carries on asking you questions until you drop your guard and say 'yes' or 'no'.

You can vary this game with the first player asking a question, to which the other player has to reply with another question. If they reply with a statement they're out.

Travelling by car

In many ways, travelling by car is the easiest option with children. You don't have to worry about luggage restrictions so everyone can take their favourite things (within reason!) and you can please yourself when and where you stop on the way. Plus, if the noise levels get too high, there's no fear of disturbing anyone (apart from you, that is!).

How to keep everyone happy on the journey

• Take the scenic route rather than the fastest one. You might be determined to get to your destination as fast as possible, but ripping along a soulless motorway can be very tedious for young passengers. Try to vary your journey – it will keep you more alert and give the children plenty of inspiration for word games etc.

- Nip in the bud endless questions about the distance by challenging children to work how out how long it will take to get to your destination given your average speed. Divide the total number of miles by your average speed. So, if you're travelling 300 miles and your average speed is 50 mph, it will take six hours to reach your destination.

- If you're sharing the driving with another adult, take it in turns to sit in the back with the children to keep them from squabbling.

- Take plenty of healthy snacks. Avoid food and drinks loaded with sugar unless you want hyperactive kids bouncing around the car (and ban drinks with caffeine unless you want horribly wide-awake children). Pack plenty of water and fruit juice, as you can get very dehydrated cooped up in a car for long periods, especially if the air conditioning is on.

- If it's a hot day and the sun's pouring in, fix sun blinds on the back windows to keep passengers cool.

- Make frequent stops to refresh you and let the kids offload some energy. Resist the temptation to put in as many miles as you can without stopping. Most importantly, don't drive if you're overtired. The instant you feel yourself becoming even slightly dozy, stop at the first opportunity and take a nap. Even 15 minutes will refresh you.

- If any of your children suffer from car sickness, make sure they don't read in the car, as this can make it worse. Don't let them eat fatty foods or fizzy drinks as these can also make them feel worse. Open windows to let in fresh air and get them involved in word games where they have to look out of the car. Children prone to car sickness may also travel better in the front passenger seat.

- Don't overpack the car so your passengers are buried under a mound of stuff. Stow excess luggage on a roof rack and leave seats clear so everyone has plenty of room. Keep children comfortable with lots of pillows, blankets, even a small duvet.

- Hang organizer bags on the back of the front seats, so children can stash their stuff in them. You could also hang play trays over the front seats so they have a level surface to write and draw on.

- Keep the car tidy and free from litter. Driving with objects rolling about under your seat is distracting and dangerous.

Learn a language

The car is the perfect place for children to brush up on their language skills as there aren't any distractions and there are plenty of things to use for vocabulary. Declare that everyone has to speak French or Spanish (or any other language) for, say, ten minutes. If this idea goes down like a lead balloon, play a language tape which your children won't be able to resist interacting with, especially if it's a fun one.

Word games

These are useful to distract children if they're prone to car sickness or getting a bit tetchy.

Number plate spelling

Each player picks a word and spells it out by finding the letters on the number plates of cars. Players take it in turns to pick a letter on the number plate of each oncoming car. You're only allowed to take one letter from a number plate at a time and you have to find the letters in the order they appear in the word. The first player who succeeds in making a word wins or you can score five points for each word, and set a time limit before you add everyone's scores up to find the winner. 'O' can be a letter or a number.

Variation

To make the game more difficult, players have to find three-letter words they can add to ones already made to form six-letter words. For example, if you have the word LAP, you can look for TOP to make LAPTOP. Set a time limit and score ten points for each six-letter word made to find the winner.

Car alphabet

Each player takes three letters on a car's number plate and makes up a sentence, phrase or names that these letters could stand for. The phrase can be as daft as you like – in fact the sillier the better. For example, ST12 0TD could stand for 'Small Turtles Organize Tiny Dances.'

A–Z

Each player has to find all the letters of the alphabet, in the right order, by looking at road signs, posters, street and house names, shop signs, billboards, car number plates, and so on. If another player is trying to find the same letter, the first person to find it and shout it out wins the letter. That doesn't necessarily mean they're going to win, as it can take a while to find a particular letter, which gives other players the chance to catch up. This is worth pointing out to younger children who might get a bit despondent that they're not winning.

Pub cricket (UK)

A game revolving around pub signs where you count the number of legs, which score as 'runs'. For instance, The Dog and Duck counts as six runs, as a dog has four legs and a duck has two. If a pub doesn't have any legs, for example, The Back of Beyond, you can't score any runs, so it's on to the next player. The winner is the player who scores the most during their turn.

Road cricket

This is a variation on Pub Cricket. You choose a colour, say red, and count every red car passing you as a run. The players pick a colour you can all be bowled out by, for example, black. Therefore, when a black car comes along, you're out, and it's the next player's turn.

Singsongs

Having a good old singsong in the car cheers everyone up instantly, even the beleaguered driver! Put on pop songs you can all join in with, play karaoke sing hymns, nursery rhymes or try these ideas:

Singing the alphabet

The first person has to sing a song beginning with the letter 'A'; the next person a song beginning with 'B'; the third person a song beginning with 'C' and so on, through the alphabet. If you can't think of a song for a particular letter you're out. (You could leave out X and Z unless you're very resourceful.)

Round songs

A round song is where people sing the same song but at different points. You begin singing a song and when you get to the second line another person begins at the first. When this second person reaches the second line another person begins, and so on. When you get to the end of the song you start all over again. Traditional songs and nursery rhymes work well as round songs, for example *London Bridge* and *Three Blind Mice*.

London Bridge

London Bridge is falling down,
Falling down, falling down,
London Bridge is falling down,
My fair lady.

Build it up with wood and clay,
Wood and clay, wood and clay,
Build it up with wood and clay,
My fair lady.

Wood and clay will wash away,
Wash away, wash away,
Wood and clay will wash away,
My fair lady.

Build it up with bricks and mortar,
Bricks and mortar, bricks and mortar,
Build it up with bricks and mortar,
My fair lady.

Bricks and mortar will not stay,
Will not stay, will not stay,
Bricks and mortar will not stay,
My fair lady.

Build it up with iron and steel,
Iron and steel, iron and steel,
Build it up with iron and steel,
My fair lady.

Iron and steel will bend and bow,
Bend and bow, bend and bow,
Iron and steel will bend and bow,
My fair lady.

Build it up with silver and gold,
Silver and gold, silver and gold,

Build it up with silver and gold,
My fair lady.

Silver and gold will be stolen away,
Stolen away, stolen away,
Silver and gold will be stolen away,
My fair lady.

Set a man to watch all night,
Watch all night, watch all night,
Set a man to watch all night,
My fair lady.

Suppose the man should fall asleep?
Fall asleep, fall asleep,
Suppose the man should fall asleep?
My fair lady.

Give him a pipe to smoke all night,
Smoke all night, smoke all night,
Give him a pipe to smoke all night,
My fair lady.

Three blind mice

Three blind mice,
Three blind mice,

See how they run!
See how they run!

They all ran after the farmer's wife,
Who cut off their tails
With a carving knife.

Did you ever see such a thing in your life,
As three blind mice.

Games to let off steam

Stop as often as you can on the way so children can offload all
their pent-up energy. Service stations often have playgrounds for
younger children, while older children can kick a football
around or play Frisbee. Try these action games to get the whole
family re-energized:

Action stations

The first player claps, the next player claps and sneezes, the next claps, sneezes and hops on one foot, the next claps, sneezes, hops on one foot and jumps, and so on. The game can go on as long as you like, with players adding new actions as they go along. The winner is the person who repeats everything correctly and adds a new action.

Simon says

A player is Simon and orders the other players to do various actions such as 'Simon says, lift up your left leg', 'Simon says turn around once', 'Simon says wave both hands in the air'. However, if the order is given without 'Simon says' being said, the players shouldn't do anything. Any player who forgets and carries out an action without the words 'Simon says' is out. The last player left in the game wins.

Travelling by coach

With air-conditioning and toilets on board, coaches are very comfortable these days, and the cheapest form of transport if you're on a budget. However, you don't have the freedom of stopping when you want, and children can find coach travel tedious if they haven't got anything to do. Try these tips to keep them distracted:

- While kids can't be as noisy on a coach as in the car, there are still plenty of games you can play with them, such as I-spy, Animal, Vegetable or Mineral, Just a Minute and Shopping List (see Brainteasers for long journeys on p. 4.)
- Some coaches have drop-down trays so you can play board games and cards easily.
- Some children don't travel well on long coach journeys. Give your child a travel-sickness tablet before setting out if you think it might be a problem.
- Check how much luggage you can take on the coach before you travel. The coach should have overhead lockers where you can stash personal items.
- Personal stereos and MP3 players are perfect for coach travel. Children can listen to audio tapes or their favourite tracks without disturbing anyone.
- While many coaches have vending machines on board selling drinks, they're not usually the healthiest, so take plenty of water and sugar-free drinks.

Travelling by train

Children love travelling by train – the novelty of having food and drink served on board; of being able to walk about while the train hurtles through an ever-changing landscape. Taking the train is also much less stressful for parents – you don't have the worry of driving or getting lost and the kids have more space to move around in, unless it's very crowded.

Tips for train journeys

- Book your trip well in advance to get the best seats and cheapest fares. Avoid travelling during commuter hours unless you want to battle your way through hordes of irritable, weary workers.
- Don't overburden yourself with tons of luggage. Remember you have to lug it on and off the train, plus find room to stow it on board. Try to get everything in one suitcase and put things you need immediately in a small holdall or rucksack. Children can also take their own travel bags but make sure they don't forget these when you leave the train.
- Take plenty of food and drink as dining cars/buffet bars might not always be open.
- Take a travel pillow and blanket if you have room so kids can snuggle down and sleep.

Games to play on the train

Although travelling by car gives you a lot more independence, when it comes to keeping the kids amused, trains often have the edge. For a start, travel-sickness is unlikely to be a problem as trains offer a smoother ride, so children can get engrossed in their favourite books without going green. There are also a lot more games you can play on trains. As well as word games (see Brainteasers for long journeys on p. 4), board games, paper and pencil games and card games are all great ways to wile away the time. If you can, book seats with a table so everyone can spread themselves out and you have a surface to play games on.

Paper and pencil games

Alphabet sentences

Everyone has to write a sentence where every word starts with a letter from the alphabet. The letters have to be in sequence, and every word scores one point. For example, using the consecutive letters ABCDEFG you could make the sentence 'Avoid Big Cats Dancing Every Friday Going Home', which would score eight points. The sentence has to make some sort of sense no matter how daft it is. A player can start on any letter you wish. The game works best if you set a time limit, say five minutes, for everyone to come up with a sentence. The game ends when a player reaches a total of 50 points, or you could just play a certain number of rounds, and total the scores at the end to find the winner.

Battleships (2–4 players)

This game usually involves two players although you could have four people playing in teams of two. Each player (or side) draws a square divided into 36 smaller squares (six by six), labelling the squares 1 to 6 on the top line, and A to F down the side, so they can be identified by their letter and number (see figure 1).

figure 1 the grid for Battleships

Each player also has a fleet of battleships:

- 1 aircraft carrier (10 points)
- 2 destroyers (5 points each)
- 2 submarines (3 points each)
- 3 minesweepers (1 point each)

Both players then place each of their battleships in one of the squares, marking its position with a letter: A=aircraft carriers; D=destroyers; S=submarines; M=minesweepers.

The battle starts and players take it in turns to fire at each other. The first player calls out a grid number, for example E2 or B4. If his enemy has a battleship in that square, he has sunk it and wins points.

Each player can fire 12 rounds. At the end of the battle the players add up the points for each battleship they have sunk. The one with the most points is the winner.

Boxes (up to 4 players)

Draw a grid of dots on a sheet of paper. This can be as big or small as you want the game to last. Each player takes turns drawing a line between two dots. The lines must be horizontal or vertical (not diagonal) and between two dots next to each other. If a player completes a square, they put their initials inside it, and win another turn. The player with the most squares when all the dots are joined wins.

Dots (2 or more players)

Each player draws 15 dots at random on a sheet of paper and then swaps the sheet with another player. With a time limit of, say, ten minutes, everyone has to make a recognizable picture by joining up the dots. You can add extra features to finish off your picture.

Hangman (2 or more players)

One player, acting as the 'hangman', has to think up a word, for example, 'pencil', and marks six dashes on a piece of paper to represent the word. The other players each guess a letter in turn. If they guess a letter that's in the word, the hangman puts it in the right place on one of the dashes. So, if a player guesses 'P', the hangman would write:

$$P \_ \_ \_ \_ \_$$

However, if a player makes a wrong guess and says 'S', for example, the hangman draws one line of the gallows. For every wrong guess he adds another line, as shown in figure 2.

Play continues this way until someone guesses the word or the hangman finishes building the gallows.

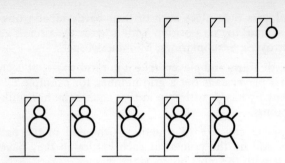

figure 2 Hangman gallows

Picture consequences (2–4 players)

Everyone is given a sheet of paper. At the top of the page, you draw a head (the sillier the better), letting the lines of the neck extend down below the fold. Now fold the paper down to hide your drawing but leaving the lines of the neck visible. Everyone then passes on their sheet to the next player. Using the neck lines as a guide, each player draws a body, including shoulders, arms and hands, in the middle of the paper. Swap sheets of paper once again. Now fold the paper down to hide your drawing but leaving the leg lines visible then draw the legs and feet, fold the paper down and pass to the next player. You all unfold your drawings and have a good laugh. If you want four people to play, the feet can be drawn as a separate item.

Noughts and crosses (Tic Tac Toe in US)
(2 players)

Younger children will enjoy this easy game, where the aim is to get a line of noughts or crosses. Draw two horizontal lines and two vertical lines crossing them, as shown in figure 3. Decide who is 'noughts' and who is 'crosses' and then take it in turns to place a nought or a cross in a square. The winner is the person who manages to get a row of crosses or noughts, either diagonally, down or across.

Travelling by plane

These days a great deal of family holidays will involve some sort of plane journey. Flying with children can be much more relaxing than other types of transport – it's (relatively) quick,

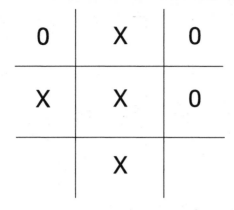

figure 3 Noughts and crosses

there's no chance of being stuck in traffic jams and someone else is at hand to provide your children with refreshments. However, long-haul flights can be a challenge, especially for younger children. Asking them to sit still and behave for hours on end is a tall order. Then there's the dreaded airport delay – stuck in the departure lounge for hours on end waiting for your flight to be announced, while the children go slowly mad with boredom. As always, when taking children on trips, be prepared for delays by making sure you pack things for them to do.

Tips for plane journeys

- If you're going on a long-haul flight, comfortable seats are a must, especially if you've got children with you. Seat pitch – the distance between your seat and the one behind – can vary considerably between one airline and another. An extra couple of inches of pitch can make all the difference, and means that your knees won't be jammed up against the seat in front.
- Bulkhead seats (the bulkhead is the partition that divides the plane into sections) are popular with families as they have more legroom, but the armrests don't always go up in these seats so children can't sprawl out easily. You also might find it annoying that the tray tables are usually stored in the armrests and you can't stow bags under bulkhead seats.
- Find out what sort of in-flight entertainment is provided – the better it is, the quieter your children will be! Ask about

personal video screens and whether there are personal ports to plug in your DVD player – both good distractions.

- If you're flying with an American airline visit **www.seatguru.com** where you can compare seating plans and in-flight facilities for all the major US airlines.

- Allow plenty of time to get to the airport, and check in as early as possible. Tightened security measures can mean long delays at the check-in so be prepared for a long wait before boarding your plane.

- If you're flying with more than one child, avoid arguments about who gets the window seat by booking two windows in front of each other so one parent sits beside each child. Alternatively, get them to agree to swap seats halfway through the journey.

- Check with the airline before departure about what you can and can't take on the plane. Warn your children in advance about security in airports and what to expect. And make sure clever teenagers don't make any jokes about bombs – no one will find it funny.

- Make sure you have plenty of healthy snacks, and ensure everyone drinks lots of water as planes are very dehydrating. Take a facial water spray for faces.

Boredom busters

If your flight is delayed, pacifying fractious children in a packed airport lounge can try the patience of the most saintly parent. If you've got hours to kill, keep children distracted with the following suggestions:

- Before you go through passport control, take the children to the spectator's gallery to watch planes taking off.

- Take younger children to a play area where they can offload some energy. Most airports have these and they're usually free.

- Retreat to a paying lounge. Most of the UK's airports have executive lounges which welcome families as well as business travellers. Heathrow Airport, for instance, has a paying lounge in each terminal equipped with games, toys, TV and video games. US airports also offer an impressive range of facilities for families.

- Play board games, cards, quizzes – anything to keep everyone happy and whinge-free!

02

days out: where to take the kids

In this chapter you will learn:
- what to do in town
- about beach games and activities including fossil hunting, building sandcastles and exploring rock pools
- about family activities in the countryside.

If you're planning to take the kids out for the day, you'll find a huge range of activities on offer, and you don't have to travel far to find them. In England, you're never far away from a beach, where the family can while away hours fossil hunting, pottering around rock pools or just messing about on the beach. Towns offer a wealth of activities from playgrounds to museums, swimming pools to art galleries. Or take a trip out to the countryside by train or, even better, cycle there. Take a picnic and get your children to really see what's around them.

Around the town

Wherever you live, you're bound to find plenty of activities and events geared towards children in your neighbourhood. Find out what's on offer by contacting your local tourist office, looking in your local paper or checking out the library noticeboard. The internet is also a mine of information for local events. Just click on the area you live in and you should find a whole host of options to keep children occupied.

Sports centres

It's not hard to find a sport or activity close to home that will suit you and your children. From swimming to basketball, football to fencing, there's something for everyone. Book yourselves in for a session at the local pool, take them ice skating, go bowling or try something new with the children such as yoga, salsa, martial arts or horse riding. However, it's important to choose an activity that you will enjoy yourself. If you're not happy about the idea of ice skating, for instance, let a friend take the kids, and you can be a happy spectator without the bruises!

Swimming is one of the best activities for all-round fitness. It tones the whole body, improves stamina and doesn't put any strain on joints. It's also something the whole family can take part in. Whether your child needs to learn to swim or you want to improve on your own swimming skills, you'll find a course to meet your needs. You could also think about enrolling yourself and/or your children in a lifesaving course.

Places of culture

Given the choice, children would much rather watch a video rather than do something 'cultural', but prise them away from the TV and you'll be surprised at how much they'll enjoy visiting museums and galleries. Many of these places put on free concerts and activities for children, so find out what special events are going on.

Museums

Once upon a time museums were dull, morgue-like places, where people spoke in hushed tones and children weren't allowed to touch any of the exhibits. These days it's a different story. Museums bend over backwards to welcome children and engage their interest with interactive displays, educational programmes and special events in the holidays. Even better, museums in Britain are free, although you have to pay for special exhibitions.

Art galleries and arts centres

Encourage your children to appreciate art in all its myriad forms by taking them to a variety of exhibitions and galleries. Don't make a big deal about it or feel obliged to deliver mini lectures on the merits of various artists. Instead, focus on one or two paintings or sculptures and ask your children what they like about them. Younger children especially respond to very bright colours and subject matters they can relate to.

Libraries

Like museums, libraries have undergone a transformation over the past few years and have been striving to attract children with talks, events and exhibitions. Foster a love of books in your children by making frequent trips to your local library. Point out books they might enjoy and that coincide with their interests.

Parks and gardens

If you don't have a big garden or aren't very keen on your kids trampling over your prized flowers, public parks are a real godsend. Many of them have playgrounds for younger children, and sports facilities for older ones. Even if they don't, just having a wide, open space where kids can play football or simply run around and let off steam is invaluable (see Chapter 07 for ideas for activities). Take a picnic in the summer along with a football or Frisbee and make a day of it.

Zoos and aquariums

Animals hold a special fascination for children and visits to zoos are an excellent way for them to learn about different animals and their habitats. Modern zoos are intimately linked with conservation and work hard to inform and educate children about the plight of endangered species. Many also offer 'encounter' sessions where children can meet different types of animals and ask the keeper questions about them.

Out of town

This is where you'll find all the big attractions for families – theme parks, adventure trails, wildlife parks, nature reserves and more. If you're looking for a birthday treat or something special, these make brilliant family days out. Theme parks, particularly, can be costly, especially if you're taking a large group, so find out about special deals and money-off vouchers. Food can be quite pricey too, so you might want to take your own drinks and healthy snacks.

On the beach

Chill out, play a game, hunt for shells or go on a fossil hunting expedition – beaches are the perfect place to spend some quality family time (and come home with change in your pocket).

Fossil hunting

This is one of the most fascinating activities you can enjoy as a family. The thrill of finding a dinosaur footprint or the remains of a creature which existed millions of years ago is second to none, and it's an experience your children won't forget. The good news about fossil hunting is that as well as being educational, free and fun, you don't need to spend a fortune on expensive equipment to find them – most fossils are just lying there, waiting to be found. Waterproofs and Wellington boots are all you need, plus patience and an eagle eye. Some areas yield fossils very quickly; others take more time.

Where to find fossils

Fossils are remains or traces of creatures which lived thousands or even millions of years ago. They come in all types and sizes, from bones and shells to footprints and worm trails. You'll find most fossils in sedimentary rock, which is found all over the world. The best places to look for fossils include beaches and cliffs, quarries and road cuttings. The beach is a particularly rich source as the constant pounding of waves against the cliffs has the effect of dislodging fossils on to the beach. Your local museum should also be able to tell you what type of fossils you can find in your area.

Make sure you know the rules about fossil hunting in your area. Some sites forbid the use of hammers; in most places you can only collect fossils if you find them lying around on the beach.

Safety note
Keep these guidelines firmly in mind when you're looking for fossils with your family:

- Be very careful where you and your children hunt for fossils. Keep away from cliffs and crumbling rocks.
- Always check the weather forecast and times of tides before setting out.
- Keep an eye on the time when you're fossil hunting. It's easy to become so engrossed that you don't notice the tide coming in.

You will need:
- small trowel or knife to prise fossils from clay
- pocket guide to identify fossils
- map of the area
- paper and pen to record finds
- kitchen towel or newspaper to wrap fossils in
- strong bag to carry fossils in

Avoid using hammers to dislodge fossils. They're dangerous as chips can fly in your face, as well as being harmful to the environment. Overuse of hammers by fossil hunters has caused a lot of damage to geological sites.

Common animal fossils
Ammonites These marine creatures first appeared around 400 million years ago and became extinct 65 million years ago, when they died out along with the dinosaurs. They belong to a group of predators known as cephalopods, which includes the octopus and squid.

Bivalves (clams, oysters, mussels and their relatives) These have been going strong for over 500 million years and are still plentiful today.

Brachiopods (lamp shells) One of the most common fossils, these marine animals resembling clams have lived in the ocean for over 600 million years.

Corals Marine animals related to sea anemones and jellyfish, that have thrived for over 450 million years.

Crinoids Called sea lilies because they look like plants, crinoids feed by filtering out plankton and are among the oldest fossils on Earth.

Echinoids Marine creatures closely related to starfish, sea cucumbers, sea lilies and brittle-stars.

Gastropods (or snails) These have existed in the sea for over 500 million years. Several hundred million years ago they also transferred into freshwater and on to land.

Trilobites First appearing 600 million years ago, these famous and much studied hard-shelled segmented creatures were the earliest known animals to possess sight. They evolved into all sorts of beautiful and strange forms but became extinct about 245 million years ago.

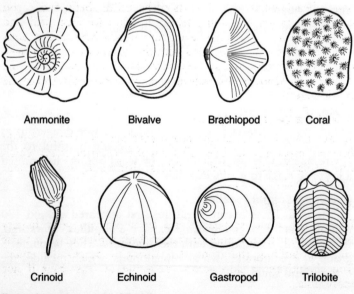

| Ammonite | Bivalve | Brachiopod | Coral |

| Crinoid | Echinoid | Gastropod | Trilobite |

figure 4 common animal fossils

Four fun things to do on the beach

1 Go beachcombing

A fascinating, totally free, pastime for all the family, which involves searching the beach for unusual objects washed up on the strandline. At first glance you might not see very much, but look closely among all the rubbish, especially after a heavy storm, and you'll find all manner of intriguing objects yielded up by the sea. Marine life found by beachcombers on the English coast in 2007 included dead fish and fish skeletons, dead jellyfish, dolphins and porpoises, cuttlefish, mermaid's purses (egg cases of the dogfish), starfish, violet sea snails, barnacles and crabs. Even man-made rubbish can be surprisingly interesting. Take a stick to gently search for treasures and a bag to put them in.

> **Safety note**
> Make sure you all wear proper shoes and keep a close eye on younger children. Always make sure that you go beachcombing when the tide is out – check the times of the tides before you set out to be on the safe side.

2 Collect shells and pebbles

Sandy beaches harbour all sorts of beautiful shells, while you can spend hours searching pebble beaches for beautiful and unusual stones. You might even find fossils here. See if your children can match up pebbles with the types of rock in nearby cliffs. If they don't match, they may have been brought by the tide or even deposited by melting glaciers towards the end of the last ice age.

3 Make a beach sculpture

Create a work of art on the beach with natural objects. Sandy beaches, especially, harbour all sorts of fascinating items which can be used such as shells, pebbles, driftwood, seaweed and clean rubbish.

4 Skim stones

Find a flat stone or pebble and lay it flat on your fingers between your thumb and forefinger. With a flick of your wrist and still holding the stone flat, throw it across the water. You should see it skip across the water at least four if not more times.

Top ten beachcombing sites in Britain

Runswick Bay, North Yorkshire
Newgale Beach, Pembrokeshire
Westward Ho! Beach, Devon
Cowes, Isle of Wight
Camber, East Sussex
Frinton Beach, Frinton on Sea, Essex
Herne Bay East, Kent
Barmston, East Yorkshire
Combe Martin Beach, Devon
Cresswell Dunes & Foreshore, Northumberland

How to build the best sandcastle

The secret to a perfect sandcastle is to keep the sand wet while you're making it. However, don't let it get waterlogged – the golden rule is eight parts water to one part sand or enough to bind the particles of sand together.

Sandcastles are delicate structures so you need a light touch when you're carving designs or making modifications. Plastic cutlery can make excellent modelling tools – use plastic spoons to remove excess sand; plastic knives to shave or carve out stairs; plastic forks to create interesting textures on walls and towers. Plastic straws are also handy for drawing patterns on your castle.

Safety note

Kids can get so absorbed in their sandcastles that they can easily get sunburnt without realizing it. Make sure everyone slathers on sunscreen and wears T-shirts and hats if it's very hot.

You will need:

- spray bottle to keep sand wet
- buckets and other plastic containers
- strong spades for digging
- plastic spoons, knives, forks and straws for modelling.

Step 1 Decide on the design of your sandcastle and where you're going to build it. Choose a site far enough away from the water to stop it getting washed away. It's worth digging a trench to let sea water in, to save you endless walks to the water.

figure 5 a sandcastle to aspire to

© Manuel Abadia, 2008

Step 2 Build the platform or base of your castle. Soak the site with several buckets of water and add a large pile of sand at least one metre (three feet) high. Keep soaking it with water and press down firmly, creating a platform.

Step 3 Build the towers, starting with a central one in the middle of the platform. This is the biggest, tallest tower and is best built with your hands. Make a flat, round patty, several inches thick, out of very wet sand. Place it in the middle of your platform. Make another smaller patty and place this on top of the first. Continue in this way until you're happy with the height and shape of your tower. It should be broad at the bottom and taper towards the top.

Step 4 Make walls to link the towers. Take a handful of wet sand, press your hands together to squeeze out excess water and put the wedge of sand in place to make a wall. Make another wedge to place next to it and carry on until the wall is complete. The walls need to be strong and thick, and if you're building high ones, they need to be broad at the base and gradually taper as they get higher.

Step 5 Make an arch by tunnelling through the base of a wall, taking care the wall doesn't collapse when you're doing this. Gently enlarge and shape the opening to make an arch, using a plastic knife to shave off excess sand.

Step 6 Build ramps in the same way as the walls. You can adapt ramps into walkways or moats around your sandcastle, or into staircases by carving out stairs with a plastic knife.

Step 7 Decorate the sandcastle with shells, pebbles, feathers, strands of seaweed, coloured plastic – anything you find on the beach that appeals to you.

Beach games

Beaches are great places to play all sorts of family games such as Frisbee, football, soccer, baseball, French cricket (see Chapter 07) and beach volleyball (see p. 31). Give yourself plenty of space, and keep well away from other people.

Water battle

All you need for this are heavy-duty water guns and a beach ball. Divide everyone into two teams and draw lines in the sand to represent two zones. Use the water guns to squirt the ball into your zone and keep your opponents from squirting it into theirs.

Buried treasure

This is best played on a quiet beach with plenty of space – sunbathers won't take kindly to kids rooting around them for treasure. Put some small treats inside a 'treasure chest' (this can be an old shoebox covered in tin foil) and bury it in the sand. Remember where you've put it though. Draw a treasure map with clear landmarks and an X marking the spot for the buried treasure. The landmarks should be easy to find, but don't make the treasure hunt too easy or the children will lose interest. You can also add things like 'Walk ten steps forward and ten steps sideways' to add to the intrigue, but make it clear where they have to do this, or the treasure hunters could end up in the sea!

Beach darts

Draw a big dartboard in the sand with a stick (use figure 6 to help you). It doesn't have to be a perfect replica – you can just draw a very basic shape with lines radiating from the centre and numbers on each zone. Throw shells or pebbles at the 'board'. Set a limit, say, the first person to reach a score of 50 or 100 is the winner.

figure 6 a standard dartboard

King of the ring

Boys especially will relish this rough and tumble game. Draw a large circle in the sand. Everyone stands inside the circle and you have to push, shove and wrestle the other people out of the circle. The last player left in the ring earns the title King of the Ring.

Beach volleyball (4 players or more)

Hugely popular all over the world, beach volleyball is recognized as an Olympic sport although you can play your own more relaxed version of it as long as there's space on the beach. It's a very active sport with lots of jumping, so it's great for boosting the whole family's fitness.

To play it you need a volleyball and a net (if you don't have a proper net you can use windbreaks or a badminton net). It's usually played with two teams of two players each, although you can play with more people if you want. The aim of the game is to send the ball over the net so it hits the ground in your opponents' court, and to prevent your opponents doing the same in your court. Normally the court should be eight metres (26 feet) square with a 'free zone' five to six metres (16 to 19 feet) wide around the outside of the court. If the ball lands in the free zone it's out of bounds, but players can go into it during play.

Flip a coin to see who serves first. You serve by hitting the ball with your arm or hand into your opponents' court and they have to return it in the same way. You can't catch or throw the ball but it can touch any part of the body above the waist. You win points by hitting the ball into the other team's court which they are unable to return or when the other team breaks a rule. The first team to reach 25 points wins the set and the first to win three sets wins the match. Each team can have up to three touches to return the ball (hitting the ball to another teammate) and this includes touching the ball by mistake. If you touch the ball, you can't touch it again, until another teammate or an opponent touches it.

Exploring rock pools

Exploring the mysteries of rock pools is one of the delights of childhood. Go down to the beach at low tide, find some rocks and start poking around. Everyone needs to wear waterproof shoes with non-slip soles as the rocks can be very slippery. Don't go barefoot as many rocks have sharp surfaces. Always check the tide times before you set off to avoid any danger of getting cut off by the incoming tide.

What you may find

Anemones These live on rocks and use their tentacles to trap food such as shrimps. They are delicate creatures so shouldn't be poked or kept out of water.

Barnacles Resembling limpets, barnacles attach themselves to rocks. At low tide they look like shells but when the tide comes in they put out tiny feathery limbs to trap plankton.

Crabs These are usually found lurking under rocks foraging for food.

Fish When the tide goes out fish can get stranded in rock pools.

Limpets Rocks are usually covered with limpets, which use their large, muscle 'foot' to cling on for all they're worth (hence the phrase 'clinging like a limpet'). They creep over the rocks, living off weed. They shouldn't be prised off rocks, but left undisturbed.

Seaweed This provides shelter and sustenance to masses of tiny creatures. Look underneath to see what you can spot, but always put seaweed back exactly as it was or the creatures dependent on it won't survive.

Starfish These are rarely seen in rock pools but if you're lucky enough to find one don't touch it.

> Make sure all rock pool creatures are put back where they were found. If rocks and stones are overturned, they should be put back just as they were. Any creatures put in jars or buckets of water should be put back where they came from as quickly as possible.

Pond dipping

Children love messing about in ponds, and pond dipping is an activity younger children find especially exciting – trawling a net through the water to catch all sorts of mini-beasts. Pond dipping involves taking creatures out of a pond, observing them and then putting them back. Not only are you getting your kids out into the fresh air with this absorbing activity, but you're teaching them about the creatures that ponds harbour.

You will need:

- a net for catching pond animals
- transparent containers to hold them in
- a magnifying glass to look at them closely
- a notebook and pen to make notes.

> **Safety note**
> Always supervise young children near water and ensure they wear rubber boots as it can be slippery and muddy around ponds.

How to pond dip

Pond dipping can scare creatures in the water so take care to do it slowly and gently. Look to see what there is in the water, then fill a jar with pond water. Sweep your net through the water and transfer any netted creatures to your container, immersing the net in the water to release them. Don't pick up any of the creatures and always keep them in water. Once you have inspected your catch, taken a photo of it or made notes or a drawing, return the creatures to the pond as quickly as you can.

What you might find

Depending on the time of year you may be able to spot frogspawn, tadpoles, frogs, newts, whirligig beetles, pond skaters, dragonflies, water boatmen, great diving beetles, water lice, water scorpions, mayflies, damselflies, freshwater shrimps, ram's horn snails, great pond snails, leaches, flatworms, water mites, water flies and even small fish such as sticklebacks.

In the countryside

Announce a family outing to the countryside and your children probably won't exactly jump at the idea. If you live in a town or city, they're more comfortable with shops, roads and traffic than peaceful green spaces. Even if the countryside's on your doorstep, they would most likely prefer to play on their PlayStation than engage with nature. However, a day out in the country doesn't have to mean just going for a boring walk (as the children might view it). There are lots of activities you and your children can enjoy out of town and listed below are some ideas for family outings.

Head for a national park

From rugged coastlines to ancient woodlands, the UK's 14 national parks have something for everyone. There are masses of family activities on offer in the parks, including climbing, mountain biking, nature walks, horse riding and bird watching. Visit **www.nationalpark.org.uk** for more information.

National parks are hugely popular in the US as well, comprising 391 areas covering over 84 million acres in almost every state. These areas include national parks, monuments, battlefields, historic sites, lakeshores, seashores, recreation areas, scenic rivers and trails, and the White House. Visit **www.nps.gov** to find out more.

Take a bike ride

Cycling in the countryside is much less stressful than cycling in the town, and perfect for the whole family, including younger children. Find out about cycling routes from one of the many cycling organizations or check on the internet. Before you leave, make sure all the bikes are in good working order, test the brakes and pump up tyres if necessary, and make sure all the family wear safety helmets.

Have a picnic in a field

Kids adore the novelty of eating outdoors, and picnicking in a beautiful spot in the countryside is one of those simple family pleasures that your children will long remember.

> **Safety note**
> Always keep to public footpaths and don't stray onto private farmland or you could attract the unwelcome attention of livestock. Remember to always shut any farm gates you pass through as designated paths. Visit **www.ramblers.org.uk** if you're not sure where you can go, and for information about good walks in your area.

Camp out under the stars

Pop-up tents and instantly inflatable airbeds make camping a lot easier than it used to be. Take a tiny stove and cook out under the stars – the kids will be ecstatic. Visit **www.camp-sites.co.uk** for information about where to stay. For America, visit **www.gocampingamerica.com** for a state-by-state guide to campsites of all types.

Go on a nature ramble

Encourage your children to open their eyes and see what's around them in the countryside. Get them to spot five different wildflowers, five different birds, five different trees, five different leaves etc. Take pocket identification guides with you so you can appear knowledgeable when they ask what something is.

Try bark rubbing

Place a sheet of paper over the bark of a tree, fixing it with Blu-tack. Remove the paper covering from a wax crayon, and holding it lengthways, rub gently over the bark in one direction. Continue rubbing until a pattern emerges. Smooth barks tend to produce more striking rubbings than rough ones. To make it more interesting, get children to make bark rubbings of three different trees and compare the different patterns.

Have a go at brass rubbing

Brass rubbing involves placing a sheet of paper over a monumental brass and rubbing the paper with a wax crayon until an impression appears. Dating back to the thirteenth century and found in many English churches, monumental brasses are metal plates designed to commemorate important people. They are often cut into figure shapes and are beautifully engraved.

Before you carry out any brass rubbing, always ask permission from the church out of respect. There may be a fee involved. Some of the bigger churches may supply brass rubbing equipment, if not you will need to bring along your own kit so check this beforehand.

You will need:
- duster
- roll of strong paper
- scissors
- masking tape
- brass rubbing stick (black heelball on white paper works best)
- soft brush and dustpan.

figure 7 a brass rubbing

Dust over the memorial brass and then fix your paper over it with the masking tape. Feel over the paper to find the outline of the brass, then, using a brass rubbing stick, lightly rub it over the paper until an impression of the brass appears. Remove your brass rubbing carefully, brush up any debris and give the brass a final polish with the duster.

Conkers (2 players)

A boisterous game which children have been playing in England since the nineteenth century. The rules are very simple: two players have to try and smash each other's conker. To play, you first need some conkers. These are the seeds of horse chestnut trees which drop from trees in England in early autumn. Open the green, prickly shell and you'll find a shiny brown nut, which is a conker. Prepare the conker for your game by drilling a hole in it and threading string through it (definitely a job for an adult). Secure the string so the conker doesn't fall off. For an extra tough conker you can soak it in vinegar or bake it in the oven.

Toss a coin to see who starts. If your opponent wins the first hit, stand holding your conker out at arm's length so it's hanging down, wrapping the string around your hand to secure it. You must hold your conker still and your opponent can dictate how high you should hold the conker. Your opponent wraps the string around his or her fingers, pulls it tight and whacks their conker down on your conker. If the strings get snarled up the first player to shout 'String' has another go. If you drop your conker or it's knocked out of your hand your opponent can

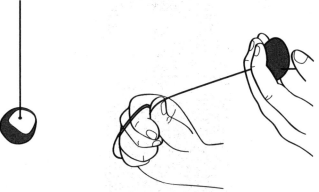

figure 8 hold your conker perfectly still and wait for the other conker to smash it

shout 'Stamps' and stamp on it. If you shout 'No stamps' you can stop your poor conker being destroyed. Play continues until one of the conkers is smashed.

How to score

If your conker is new and it smashes another new conker, it scores one point, and is called a 'one-er'. If it smashes another new conker in the next game, it's called a 'two-er' and so on. If your two-er is smashed in the next game, and another new conker wins, that conker becomes a three-er, scoring one point for itself and taking two from your conker. Scoring continues in this way. If the conker that smashed it had already won other games, the total scores of both conkers are awarded to the winner.

Safety note

Conkers can be quite a savage game so be prepared for damaged knuckles! Always make sure you hold your conker at arm's length to avoid being hit by your opponent's conker.

And something every child should know... how to make grass squeal

Pick a long, thick blade of grass, making sure it's clean. Interlace your fingers and hold the grass between the sides of your thumbs. Press on it gently so you're stretching it. Blow on the blade through the gap between your thumbs and you should hear a strange, high-pitched noise, rather like a kazoo.

03

rainy days

In this chapter you will learn:
- how to create a games box
- how to play card games with your kids, including Go fish, Crazy eights, Spit and Gin rummy
- how to play dice games
- how to make a fortune-teller, paper plane, pompon and coconut ice.

It's bucketing down outside and you're stuck indoors with a load of noisy, restless children demanding to be entertained. It's tempting just to let them veg out in front of the TV, so you can get on with those million and one jobs that can't wait. But while they'd be perfectly happy channel-hopping or zapping monsters on a video screen, you know that if you give in to their demands, by the end of the day you'll have a bunch of irritable, grumpy children on your hands.

Alternatively, you can ban all screens for the day and get your children to amuse themselves, with a bit of help from you. They might moan and groan at the suggestion that they play cards, get out a board game and, heavens above, make something, but after the initial shock of no TV you'll be surprised at how much they – and you – will enjoy yourselves. Even better, it won't cost you a penny.

All the activities mentioned here will keep your kids occupied for an hour or even an afternoon. In Chapter 09 you'll find ideas for bigger projects which take up more time.

Keep a games box

To save time hunting for games and puzzles etc., keep everything in one place, so you can instantly find things for the children to do if they're grumbling about being bored. Obviously every family will have their favourites, but here are some ideas about what to include.

Jigsaw puzzles Highly addictive, these can keep the family absorbed for hours. The best thing about puzzles is that you can return again and again to one in progress. Choose a large puzzle with plenty of interesting features – doing a jigsaw with acres of sky or water can be very tedious and the kids will lose interest. Use a side table or a tray to make the jigsaw on, and put it somewhere where it can't get knocked over.

Classic board games Games such as Scrabble, Monopoly, Trivial Pursuit, Cluedo (Clue in the US) and Pictionary never lose their appeal. Newer popular board games include Settlers of Catan, Ticket to Ride and HeroScape. Younger children love Snakes and Ladders (Chutes and Ladders in the US) and Tiddlywinks.

Other games Pass the Pigs and Boggle are two inexpensive family games that are well worth getting. Pass the Pigs is an addictive dice game, where, instead of dice, you roll tiny little pigs, and gain points according to how they fall. Boggle is a wordsearch game, where you have three minutes to find as many words as you can in a tray filled with 16 letter dice.

Playing cards Get your children hooked on cards and they'll never be at a loss as to what to do. Card games are also an excellent way for children to hone their numeracy skills and to help them think tactically and logically. Also include all the proprietary card games such as Snap, Happy Families, Uno, Old Maid and other family favourites.

Lego Every family has a box of Lego lurking somewhere in the cupboard. It's one of those toys that kids never seem to grow out of and it can keep even older children surprisingly absorbed.

Easy card games

Playing cards is a perfect activity for rainy days. There's such a wide range of games to choose from that children are bound to find one to suit, plus it's something the whole family can share in. Teach your children to play cards and you'll be giving them a skill that will benefit them enormously. It will help their mental arithmetic, encourage them to think tactically and improve their concentration. They'll also learn the value of taking turns, and how to be a good loser. Most importantly perhaps for parents, card-playing doesn't involve batteries or screens!

Common card-playing terms

The sequence of cards is Ace, 2, 3, 4, 5, 6, 7, 8, 9, 10, Jack, Queen, and King (although sometimes an Ace can be 'high' and follow after a King).

Deal One player – the dealer – gives out or deals cards to players. Play goes clockwise for games from North America, North and West Europe and Russia; anti-clockwise for South and East Europe and Asia, also for Swiss games and all Tarot games.

Face value What a card is worth in terms of numbers.

Hand The cards dealt to a player.

Stock The cards not dealt out.

Suit One of the four sets of cards which make up a pack of cards. Each set consists of 13 cards printed with Spades, Hearts, Diamonds or Clubs.

Upcard The first card turned up after the cards have been dealt out, to start play or a discard pile.

Wild card A card or cards nominated by the holder to represent any other card.

How to shuffle cards

Hold the pack face down in the palm of your right hand (or left if you're left-handed), gripping one of the short sides with your thumb, the long side with your index finger and the other short side with your middle fingers. Still holding the deck in your right hand, bring your left hand in and cradle the cards, fingers curled underneath and thumb on top. With your left thumb, draw a few cards off the deck, gripping them in your left hand and moving your right hand back. Keeping hold of the cards in your left hand, draw more cards off the top of the deck with your left thumb and drop them over the cards you hold in your left hand. Continue in this way until all the cards are in your left hand. Transfer the deck to your right hand and shuffle the cards again in the same way. Repeat a few times and you've finished.

Snap (2–6 players)

The easiest card game ever, children never tire of playing Snap because it gives them the chance to be as noisy as they like. You can play it with proper Snap cards or normal playing cards.

How to play

The dealer deals out all the cards to the players, who hold them face down, without looking at them. Starting with the dealer, each player lays one card face up on the table, making one pile. This carries on until a player lays an identical card on top of the previous one (e.g. two red Kings or two identical Snap cards).When this happens the first player to call out 'Snap' and slap their hand down on top of the cards wins and takes the pile, putting it under the cards he already holds. The winner is the first player to get all the cards in the pack.

Cheat/I doubt it (2–10 players)

The only card game where cheating is positively encouraged!

How to play

The aim of this game is to get rid of all your cards, by honest means or by cheating. Deal out all the cards in the pack – you may need to combine two packs of cards if a lot of people are playing. You play clockwise, with the first player to the left of the dealer putting a number of cards on the table and announcing what they are, for example, 'Two Queens' or 'Three 6s'. The next player has to put down cards above or below the rank, so can put down Queens, Jacks or Kings, or a 6, a 7 or a 5. However, you can lie about the cards you're putting down. You could say you're putting down two 3s, but may actually be putting down any combination of cards such as a Queen and a Jack. (It's worth remembering what cards have been laid down. If, for instance, someone has genuinely discarded two Kings, and you announce you've put down four Kings, it will be clear you're cheating if one pack is in play!)

Any of the players can challenge you and call 'Cheat' if they think you're lying. If they're right you have to pick up the cards you discarded plus the rest of the discarded pile. If you've been challenged wrongly, you have to show them the cards as proof, and the player who got it wrong has to pick up all the cards in the discard pile. You can't however challenge another player after the next player has put cards down. Play continues until one player gets rid of all their cards.

Beggar my neighbour/Strip-Jack-naked/Beat-your-neighbour out of doors (2–6 players)

A very easy game that relies on luck rather than cunning. If more than four people are playing, use two packs of playing cards, discarding the jokers.

How to play

The dealer deals out all the cards. You can't look at your cards but must hold them face down. The player to the left of the dealer puts their top card face up on the table. If the card is a numbered card (between 2 and 10), the next player puts down another card. If, however, the card is a court card (Ace, King, Queen, or Jack), the next player has to pay a forfeit by putting extra cards one by one on the pile as follows:

Ace = 4 cards
King = 3 cards
Queen = 2 cards
Jack = 1 card

If the forfeit cards are all number cards, the player who put down the court card takes the pile on the table, putting them under his or her own cards. If one of the forfeit cards is a court card the player paying the forfeit stops, and the next player has to pay a forfeit depending on the value of the court card. If the forfeit cards are all number cards, the last player to play a court card takes the cards on the table. If you have no more cards left, you're out. The game carries on and the winner is the player who ends up with all the cards.

Crazy eights (2–6 players)

A game that moves fast and relies on luck rather than skill. The aim is to get rid of all your cards. (You may also know the game as Crates, Switch, Swedish Rummy, Last One or Rockaway. In Germany it's called Mau-Mau; in Switzerland Tschausepp; in the Netherlands Pesten.)

How to play

There are lots of different variations of Crazy Eights, but in the basic game you play with a full pack of cards (or two packs if four or more are playing). If two people are playing, each player is dealt seven cards; three to four players have five cards each. Put the rest of the cards face down in the middle of the table to form a stockpile, with the top card placed face up next to it. The only thing you have to remember is that 8 is a wild card, meaning that it can be played as any card in the pack.

The player to the left of the dealer starts and play carries on clockwise. Each player has to match the card on the discard pile in suit or rank. For instance if the top card is a 3 of Spades, you have to put down a 3 or any Spade. If you don't have a card you can play, you have to draw one from the stockpile. In some versions of the game, you can play the drawn card straightaway if it's valid; in other versions, you keep on drawing until you can play, or you can carry on drawing cards up to a fixed number, after which if you still can't go, play passes to the next player. You have to lose a turn to discard any cards. However, if you have an 8, you can play it as any card. You nominate a suit and the next player has to play a card of that suit or another 8. Play carries on until a player has no cards left. If the discard pile runs out before the game is finished, shuffle it and turn it over to start a new discard pile, turning a card over and placing it face up as before. The winner is the first player to discard all of his or her cards and gets the total points of all the other cards players have left. Each 8 counts as 50; court cards count as 10; aces count as 1; and all the rest as their face value. You can also choose to play to a certain number such as 200.

Chicken feed (3 or more players)

Use an old pack of cards as this game can get quite frantic as players pounce for cards.

How to play

Spread a pack of cards face up on the table. One person – the caller – sits with his or her back turned to the cards. The caller, looking at a separate pack of playing cards, shouts out a card, for example, 'King of Diamonds', and everyone feverishly tries to spot it on the table. If you find it, you have to put your index finger on it and whizz it back to your place. Be warned – as soon as the other players see you claim the card, they will also put their fingers on the card and try to grab it for themselves. The winner is the player who manages to get the most cards.

Go fish (ideally 3–6 players but 2 can play)

You can play this with ordinary playing cards or a Go Fish pack of cards.

How to play

Two players are dealt seven cards each; three to six players are dealt five cards each. The rest of the cards are placed in a pile face down in the middle of the table.

The aim of this game is to collect sets of four cards of the same rank. To do this, you ask the other players for cards of a specific rank (but you must already hold one card of the same rank). For example, if you already hold one King, and decide to collect three more to make up a set, you ask another player, 'John, can I have your Kings?' John has to give you any Kings he may have. If he gives you one or more cards, you have another turn. You can ask any player for any rank you already hold, including the same one you just asked. If the player you asked doesn't have a card to give you, they say, 'Go fish'. You then take the top card from the pile of cards on the table.

If you draw a card of the rank you wanted, you show it to the other players and get another turn. However, if you draw a card that's not the right rank, you keep the card, and play passes to the person who said 'Go fish'.

When you collect a set of four cards of the same rank, you show the set to the other players and place it face down in front of you. The game continues until either someone has no cards left in their hand or the draw pile runs out. The winner is the player with the most sets of four cards.

Variation: specific card

Here, you ask another player for a card of specific rank and suit. You must already hold at least one card of that rank. For example: 'Susan, please give me the 6 of Clubs.' If Susan has it, she gives it to you and you have another turn. If she doesn't, she says 'Go fish' and you take a card from the pile on the table. If you draw the card you requested, you have another turn. If not, you keep the card and it's the next player's turn.

Before playing this version, you all decide whether you can ask for a card you already hold. If you do, obviously you'll be told to 'Go fish' and play passes to the next person. However, the advantage in this devious ploy is that the other players won't realize you hold that particular card, so it will help you to collect sets.

Happy families (3 or more players)

In the UK this popular card game is played with a set of picture cards, illustrating the mother, father, son and daughter of 11 families.

How to play

The aim is to collect whole families by asking the other players for cards. The dealer deals the cards and the player to the dealer's left begins. You ask another player for a card, for example, 'Please, have you got Mr Bun the Baker?' but you must already hold at least one card of the same family. If the player gives you the card, you can ask the same player or another player for another card. If the player doesn't have it, they say 'Not at home' and the turn passes to them. Players place their sets of families face down in front of themselves. Play continues until a player matches their cards into complete families. Every time you ask for a card you have to say 'Please', as in 'Please have you Miss Squirrel?' If you forget to say it, you lose your turn. When a card is given to you, you must say 'Thank you'. If you forget, the player giving you the card can ask for it back, taking care to say 'Please' and 'Thank you'.

Old maid (2–8 players)

The aim is to avoid ending up with the Old Maid if you're using a custom-made pack, or the Queen of Spades if you're using an ordinary pack of playing cards.

How to play

The dealer deals out the cards (minus the three Queens if you're using a normal set of playing cards). The players look at their cards and put any pairs aside (for example, two cards of the same rank, such as two 8s or two Jacks). The dealer starts play and offers his cards face down to the player on his left. The player takes a card and if it makes a pair puts the pair aside with the others. Play carries on clockwise, with each player offering and taking cards, until all the cards are paired up and one unlucky player is left holding the Queen of Spades or the Old Maid.

Spit (Slam in UK) (2 players)

Spit is a fun, noisy game, where players compete to get rid of their cards as quickly as possible. Cards are likely to get mangled in this race so it's best to use an old pack of cards.

How to play

Deal out 26 cards to each player. You and your opponent then use these cards to deal out five piles of cards in front of yourselves, all face down. The first pile consists of one card, the second two cards, and so on, until the fifth pile has five cards. Turn the top card of each pile face up. These are your stockpiles and you're not allowed to have more than five during the game. The 11 cards left in your hand are the 'spit cards' which you're not allowed to look at. Place these face down in front of you.

To start, you and your opponent shout 'spit' at the same time and both turn your top spit card face up, placing it in the middle of the table between the two rows of stockpiles. These two cards form the 'spit piles.'

This is when the game gets frantic. Using only one hand and moving one card at a time, you have to race to get your 15 stockpile cards onto the spit piles before your opponent does. However, you can only get rid of your cards if they're the next card in sequence, either higher or lower. If an Ace appears on a spit pile, you can play a King or a 2 on it. Ignore suits and colours – you're just looking at ranks.

When you move a card from one of your stockpiles to a spit pile, you can turn the next card in the stockpile face up. If you have less than five stockpiles, having played them onto spit piles, you can move the face-up card from another stockpile to fill the gap, and then turn the card face up beneath the one you have just moved.

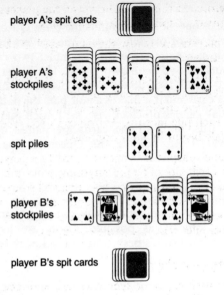

player A's spit cards

player A's stockpiles

spit piles

player B's stockpiles

player B's spit cards

figure 9 Slam/Spit/Speed

Rules

A card is officially played on a spit pile as soon as any part of that card touches the spit pile. If both players are jostling to get on the same spit pile, the player whose card touches the spit pile first wins the right to place the card. If neither of you can play from your stockpile, you both say 'spit' at the same time and turn your top spit card face up, placing it on one of the spit piles. Play carries on as before.

End of the round

A round ends when a player runs out of stock cards by playing them all, or neither player can go and both players have cards left in their stockpiles (but not their spit piles). In either situation, both players slap a spit pile with their hand, trying to slap the smaller pile. If the players slap different piles, each takes the pile they slapped. If they slap the same pile, the player whose hand is on the bottom gets that pile; the other player gets the other, bigger pile.

Both players then add any spit cards and stock cards left on their side to the spit pile that they took and shuffles their cards. The cards are then used to create a new layout as described in the set-up before. At this point, however, the players could have unequal numbers of spit cards in their hands.

When both players are ready, they say 'spit' at the same time and play continues.

If you have less than 15 cards at the end of a round, you can't deal a complete set of stockpiles. In this case, you have to deal your cards into five stockpiles as far as they will go, turning the top card on each pile face up. As you can't spit, there will only be one spit pile begun by your opponent.

When only one spit pile is being used, the first player to get rid of his stock cards doesn't take anything from the centre. His opponent takes the spit pile and his unplayed stockpile cards. If the player with no spit cards in his hand also is the one who gets rid of his stockpiles first, he wins the game. If his opponent gets rid of his stockpiles first, the game continues.

Gin rummy (2–4 players)

An easy but satisfying game requiring skill and luck, in roughly equal measure. The aim is to be the first to get rid of all your cards by collecting runs or sets of cards. A run is where you have three or four cards of the same suit following in sequence, for example, 3 of Hearts, 4 of Hearts and 5 of Hearts. A set is where you have cards of the same rank, for example, King of Hearts, King of Diamonds and King of Spades; or 3 of Spades, 3 of Clubs, 3 of Diamonds and 3 of Hearts.

How to play

Before you start, decide how many rounds you want to play, or you can play to an agreed number, for example, the first player to reach 100 is the winner. The two players take it in turn to deal out ten cards each. The next card is placed face up on the table (this is called the discard pile) with the rest of the cards face down next to it (this is called the stockpile).

You both look at your cards and decide which ones you want to collect to make a run or a set; for example, if you already have a 2 of Hearts and a 2 of Diamonds, you might decide to collect a 2 of Spades and/or a 2 of Clubs to make a set. Alternatively, if you have a 10 of Clubs and a Jack of Clubs, you might try to collect a 9 of Clubs and/or a Queen of Clubs. However, the other player might be going for the same cards so you have to watch play very closely and be prepared to change your mind about which sets or runs you're collecting.

When it's your turn, you draw a card from the stock or discard pile, though you would only draw from the discard pile if you actually wanted that card. Once you have drawn a card, decide which one you want to keep, for example, a card which can help you get a set or a run, and then get rid of a card by placing it on the discard pile. You should always have the same number of cards you started with. The other player can take the card you placed on the discard pile, or draw a card from the stockpile before deciding which card to get rid of. When you have a run or set of cards, put them on the table face up so the other player(s) can see them. You can add cards to sets or runs completed by you or the other player(s). If the stockpile is used up, turn over the discard pile to form a new one.

If your unmatched cards total ten points or less, you can end play at any time by 'knocking'. After you've picked up a card and discarded one in the usual way, knock on the table or say 'Knock'. Put your matched sets of cards on the table, and your unmatched ones next to it (unmatched cards are referred to as 'deadwood'). Your opponent then has a chance to get rid of deadwood by adding cards to your sets or runs. However your opponent can't do this if you 'go gin' (see below).

How to score

Each card is worth its face value, for example, a 3 of Diamonds scores three points, court cards score ten points each and an Ace scores one point. At the end of a round, your scores are added up. The difference between the deadwood of each player is the winner's score for that round. For example, if your deadwood total is nine, and your opponent's deadwood total is eight, you score one point (your nine points minus your opponent's eight). If you've managed to put all your cards into sets or runs, this is called 'going gin' and you score 25 points, or 20 points if your deadwood score is lower than the other player who chooses to knock. The first player to reach the target score or gain the highest score in a set amount of rounds is the winner.

Farm animals (4–8 players)

If four people are playing, you need one pack of playing cards; if more than four are playing, you need two packs.

How to play

Each player is given the name of an animal to imitate, for example, pig, sheep, cow, chicken, cat, dog, donkey, rooster.

The dealer deals out the cards, and each player puts them in a pile face down without looking at them. You begin by taking the top card from your pile and placing it face up next to your pile. Each player in turn does the same. When a card is turned up that matches any of the other cards showing, each of the two players must make the noise of the animal represented by the other player. Whoever makes the right sound first passes all his face-up cards to the other player. The winner is the player who gets rid of all his or her cards.

Dominoes

A good game for children to learn on a wet afternoon. (Suitable for 2–4 players.) There are hundreds of variations of dominoes, a UK tile game, but draw dominoes is the game most people are familiar with.

How to play draw dominoes

Place the dominoes face down on the table and mix them up. If two people are playing, each player selects seven dominoes. If three or four people are playing, each player selects five dominoes. Keep your dominoes in front of you but hidden from the other players.

The player with the highest double places it on the table. (Doubles are placed at right angles to the other dominoes.) If no one has a double, the player with the domino of the highest value starts. The next player to the left must then place a matching domino next to the first domino. For example, if the first player started the game with a double six, the next player must play a domino that has a six on it. If the player doesn't have a domino of matching value, they must pick up a domino.

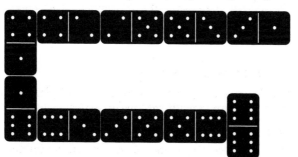

figure 10 players must match their domino with one of the numbers at either end

If they can't play the domino that they picked up from the table, they pick up another, and then a third if necessary. If they still can't go, play passes to the next player. They keep picking up dominoes until they get a playable domino. If there are no more dominoes left, the player must pass their turn.

The first person to run out of dominoes is the winner of the round. If no one runs out of dominoes but everybody passes because they don't have a playable domino, the person with the lowest score (the combined value of the dominoes they have left) is the winner. The winner scores the total number of points on all of the opponents' unplayed dominoes. If the winner has any unplayed dominoes, subtract them from the score.

How to score

A game of draw dominoes is usually played to 100 points and the scoring is kept with a pencil and paper. Some players like to use a cribbage board to keep score. In this case, the game is usually played to 121 points, which represents the final peg hole on the cribbage board.

Dice games

Games played with dice take up very little room and make great family games. (Strictly speaking, dice is the plural of 'die', but most people tend to use the word dice for the singular and the plural.)

Going to Boston (any number, but ideally 3–4 players)

You need three dice for this American game and something to shake the dice in. The first player rolls the three dice at the same time. The one with the highest number is left on the table. The two other dice are shaken and rolled, and again the one with the highest number is left on the table. The third dice is rolled and the total of the three dice is taken. This is the first player's score. Each player does the same and the person with the highest score is the winner. If two or more players have the same score, they carry on throwing until there's a winner. You can agree to play a set number of rounds with the player with the highest total score being the winner.

Twenty-one/Vingt-et-un (2 or more players)

This game requires one dice and counters or matches for each player. The players begin by putting one counter or match in the kitty or pool. Each player in turn shakes and rolls the dice as many times as they wish, aiming for a total of 21 or as close as possible. If he goes over 21 he 'busts' and is out of the game. The player with 21 or the nearest takes the kitty. It's crucial in this game to decide whether or not you're going to have another throw. If for instance your throws score you 17, it might be wise to 'stick' rather than risk going over 21. The game can carry on for a set number of rounds or a given time. The winner is the person with the most counters or matches.

Quick makes

A fortune-teller

Begin with a square-shaped piece of white paper. (To make a square, fold over one corner of the paper to the opposite edge to make a triangle. Cut across the edge of the triangle to make a square.) Fold in each corner of the paper into the middle, making a smaller square, with four folded-in triangles. Turn the paper over and repeat this action, folding in each corner so you have four folded-in triangles. Turn the paper over, fold in half, and half again, open out and there's your fortune-teller. Insert the thumb and forefinger of your right hand into two adjacent flaps and the thumb and forefinger of your left hand into the other two flaps and move the fortune-teller backwards and forwards to play.

How to use it

Flatten the fortune-teller and on each of the four top flaps write a colour, for example red, blue, green and yellow. Turn the fortune-teller over and write random numbers on the eight triangles there. Open out the triangles so you have a square with four large triangles. Divide each triangle into two with a faint pencil line, and write a prediction or fortune in each of the eight divided triangles. These could be things like 'You will be lucky today', 'You will win a prize', 'You will be rich' and so on, or they could be humorous or downright silly.

Invite a friend to find out their fortune. Place your thumbs and forefingers into the four flaps and ask them to pick a colour. Spell out the colour as you move your thumbs and index fingers

a)

Begin with a square sheet of paper.

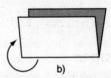

b)

Fold the piece of paper in half to make a crease, and then flatten it out.

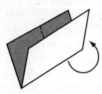

c)

Fold it in half in the other direction. Flatten the paper again – you should now have a creased cross marking the centre of the paper.

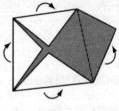

d)

In turn, fold each corner of the paper into the centre, creating four pointed flaps.

e)

Now turn the paper over, so that the flaps are pointing downwards and the square bottom is pointing towards you.

f)

In turn, fold each corner of the square bottom towards you, creating four new flaps.

g)

You should now have a smaller square. Fold this in half length-ways.

h)

Turn the square over, and push your thumbs and forefingers under the four flaps and push the corners towards the middle.

figure 11 how to make a fortune-teller

back and forth in alternating directions. Ask your friend to pick a number from the inside. Move the fortune-teller that number of times and ask them to pick a new number. Open the flap of their chosen number and read out their fortune.

A pompon

Using a compass, draw two circles on a piece of cardboard (6 centimetres/2.25 inches in diameter for a big pompon or 4 centimetres/1.5 inches in diameter for a smaller pompon). Cut a smaller hole in the middle of each circle, about half the size of the original diameter. Holding the two circles together, wind wool around the ring (using several strands at a time), until the ring is completely covered (see figure 12.a). Cut all around the outside edge between the two circles using a sharp pair of scissors (see figure 12.b). Make sure all the wool has been cut. Separate the two circles slightly, wind a length of wool between them and then tie firmly in a knot, leaving enough wool for sewing the pompon in place. Pull the two circles apart and remove, fluff out the wool to cover the centre join. Trim as desired.

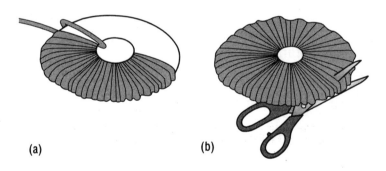

(a)   (b)

figure 12 making a pompon

Coconut ice

Ingredients
340 g (12 oz) desiccated coconut
340 g (12 oz) icing sugar
400 g (14 oz) tin of condensed milk
food colouring (optional).

Method

Place the condensed milk into a bowl and add the icing sugar. Beat well then mix in the desiccated coconut. The mixture should be thick and hard to stir but make sure everything is combined. Divide the mixture into two batches (add food colouring to one or both if you wish) and spread each coloured mixture into a 20 centimetre (8-inch) square tin to give two coloured layers. Allow to set overnight. Cut into small cubes and spread on a sheet of greaseproof paper to dry slightly.

A megaphone

You will need:

- clear tape
- one sheet of construction paper (20 × 30 centimetres/ 9 × 12 inches or larger)
- markers or crayons for decorating
- scissors (optional).

Make the paper into a cone with a large hole at one end and a small hole (about one centimetre in diameter) at the other. Hold the cone in place with tape. Cut the ends of the cone to make them even.

A paper plane

Figure 13 (a–h) (opposite) shows how to make a superior paper plane that incorporates an extra fold called the Nakamura lock, after the origami artist who originated it.

How to do invisible writing

You will need:

- lemon juice
- small paintbrush
- paper
- shallow dish.

Pour lemon juice into a shallow container. Dip the paintbrush into the juice – don't use too much – and write a message on the paper. Leave it to dry completely for a few minutes – you'll find the writing has become invisible. To read the message, place the paper on a radiator or hold it near a light bulb (but not too close or you could burn yourself and scorch the paper).

a)

Fold a sheet of paper in half lengthways. Unfold so the crease is pointing forwards.

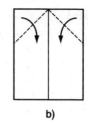

b)

Fold the top corners down to the centre crease.

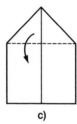

c)

Fold the tip down.

d)

Fold up about three cm of the tip. Unfold again.

e)

Fold the top corners down to the centre crease so they meet above the fold in the tip.

f)

Fold the tip up.

g)

Fold the plane in half so the tip is outside

h)

Fold the wings down and the plane is ready for take-off!

figure 13 how to make a paper plane

04

festivals and celebrations

In this chapter you will learn:
- how to make exciting crafts with your children, including a Chinese lion puppet
- how to decorate Easter eggs and make an advent calendar
- recipes to teach your children, including fortune cookies, chocolate brownies and latkes.

Celebrating seasonal events with your children is a great way to get them involved in creative activities and to learn about other customs and cultures. While most of us celebrate the obvious occasions such as Christmas, Easter and Mother's Day, there are many other equally memorable dates celebrated by other cultures and nationalities which you and your children can share. By explaining to them what the various festivals mean, you'll be helping your children develop a better understanding of other people's values. The activities don't have to be difficult or complicated either – younger children can derive huge pleasure in decorating Easter eggs, or making a Mother's Day card. Here are a few ideas of how to celebrate different festivals.

Chinese New Year (Jan–Feb)

Chinese New Year starts with the New Moon on the first day of the new year and ends on the full moon 15 days later. On New Year's Day, children and single adults are given money in red envelopes by married couples, an old custom called Hong Bao, meaning Red Packet. Then the family go from house to house greeting relatives and neighbours. The end of the New Year is marked by the Festival of Lanterns, a celebration with singing, dancing and lantern shows. The highlight of the lantern festival is the dragon dance. The dragon – which might be 30 metres long – is typically made of silk, paper, and bamboo, held aloft by young men guiding the dragon through the streets.

How to make a Chinese lion puppet

The spectacular Lion Dance is performed by two players at the start of the Chinese New Year to bring good luck. Make your own lion dance with this colourful puppet. Help younger children with the cutting out, as this involves sharp scissors.

You will need:

- construction paper in two strong colours
- coloured card
- brightly coloured tissue paper scraps
- two lolly/popsicle sticks
- glue.

To make the head and tail

Cut two oval shapes from the card. Cut a mane, eyes, nose, mouth and other decorations from tissue paper. Glue these to the head and tail.

To make the body

Cut the construction paper into strips about 2.5 centimetres (1 inch) wide. Glue two different colour strips together at right angles. Fold one strip over the other, and then repeat with the other strip, forming a concertina. Continue until you reach the end of the strips. Glue the ends together and trim off any excess (see figure 14).

To assemble your puppet

Glue a lollystick to the tail and glue the body on top. Glue the other lollystick to the back of the head and glue this to the other end of the body.

(a)　　　　　(b)

figure 14 a Chinese lion puppet
(© activityvillage.co.uk)

Fortune cookies

End a family meal with home-made fortune cookies. They're a little fiddly so children will need help making them, but they are well worth the effort. The whole family can have a go at writing the fortunes, which can be about almost anything and can be as humorous or as silly as you like! For example: 'Listen to the monkey wearing a red hat' or 'Wisdom comes from eating greens every day'.

Ingredients (makes 12)

1 egg white
drop of vanilla extract
1 pinch salt
30 g (¼ cup) unbleached, plain flour
30 g (¼ cup) white sugar.

Method

Write your fortunes on strips of white paper approximately 10 × 1 centimetres (4 × ½ inch).

Preheat the oven to 200°C/400°F, and grease two baking trays (cookie sheets). Beat the egg white and vanilla until foamy but not stiff. Sift the flour, salt and sugar together separately and fold gently into the egg white mixture.

Place a teaspoonful of the batter onto one of the prepared baking trays, and tip the tray so the batter forms a circle about 8 centimetres (3 inches) in diameter. Make two or three more cookies in this way, leaving plenty of space between them. Don't cook too many at a time as you need to shape them while they're still hot.

Bake the first sheet for about five minutes, or until the fortune cookies are golden around the edges but pale in the middle. While these are cooking, make more cookies from the batter to go on the second tray.

Once cooked, remove from the oven and quickly lift one of the cookies with a spatula and place it upside down onto a wooden board. Put the fortune in the middle of the cookie and fold the cookie in half. Place the folded edge across the rim of a cup or glass and pull the pointed edges down, one on the inside of the cup and one on the outside. Stand the folded cookies in the cups of an egg carton until they cool so they keep their shape. (By kind permission of activity.village.co.uk)

Valentine's Day 14 February – UK, USA

It's not clear exactly how Valentine's Day started. It may have originated with St. Valentine, a Roman who was martyred for refusing to give up his Christian faith. The story goes that St. Valentine left a farewell note for the gaoler's daughter and signed it 'From your Valentine'. As time went on, 14 February became the day for exchanging messages of love and St. Valentine became the patron saint of lovers.

Heart cookies

These delicious heart-shaped treats are a cross between a fairy cake and a biscuit and are very easy to make.

Ingredients (makes 24)

225 g (8 oz) self-raising flour (cake flour)
115 g (4 oz) caster sugar
100 ml (3½ fl oz) double cream (heavy cream)
½ teaspoon salt
1 egg, beaten
1 tbsp of milk
115 g (4 oz) icing sugar (confectioner's sugar)
water
few drops pink food colouring.

Method

Preheat the oven to 190°C/375°F. Line two baking sheets. Mix
the flour and sugar together. Stir in the cream, egg and enough
milk to make a stiff dough. If it gets too sticky, cover and place
in the refrigerator for about ten minutes. Roll the dough out on
a lightly floured surface until about 8 millimetres (⅓ inch) thick,
and cut into heart shapes using a small cutter. Bake for five to
eight minutes until lightly golden brown. Carefully transfer to a
wire rack to cool.

To make the icing, blend the icing sugar with a few teaspoons of
hot water (add a very little at a time) and a drop or two of pink
food colouring. Mix until smooth. Put a teaspoon of icing on
each cake and spread out with the back of a spoon. Store in an
airtight container.

From me with love

Encourage your children to make their own Valentine's Day
cards. Hopefully they might create a loving masterpiece for you.

You will need:

• white card
• felt-tip pens
• sequins
• scraps of fabric
• glue.

To make

Cut out a piece of card in the shape of a rectangle. Fold it in half
and draw your design on the front with felt-tip pens. You can
draw hearts, flowers or make a design with sequins and scraps
of fabric.

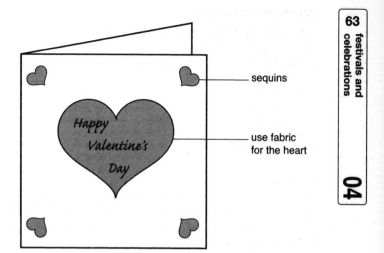

sequins

use fabric
for the heart

figure 15 encourage your children to make their own cards

Shrove Tuesday (the day before Lent)

Pancake or Shrove Tuesday is the day before the beginning of
Lent, the 40 days leading up to Easter and traditionally a time
of fasting. On Shrove Tuesday Christians would go to church
and be 'shriven' or forgiven for their sins. Since rich foods such
as eggs and fats were forbidden during Lent, one way of using
them up was to make pancakes.

As well as making pancakes on Shrove Tuesday, in some parts
of the UK people take part in pancake races, a custom arising
from a legend dating back to 1445. On Shrove Tuesday a
woman was making pancakes as the church bells rang out and,
not wanting to be late, she rushed out of the house with her
frying pan and pancake. In France and the United States,
Pancake Day is called Mardi Gras, literally 'Fat Tuesday'.

Pancakes around the world

Just about every country has its own version of the pancake.
France has thin and crispy crêpes; Russia has blinis made from
buckwheat flour; Mexico has tortillas, often with a bean or
meat filling; Greece has sweet Cretan tiganites; the Middle East
has ataif soaked in syrup; Israel has potato latkes and Ashkenazi

cheese blintzes; Morocco has semolina baghrir; and Africa has spicy chickpea and black-eye bean pancakes.

To make pancakes

Ingredients

115 g (4 oz) plain flour
pinch of salt
2 eggs
570 ml (½ pint) milk
pinch of salt.

Method

Sieve the flour and salt into a large mixing bowl. Make a well and crack the eggs into it. Add the milk and whisk until smooth: the mixture should resemble thin cream. Melt a knob of butter in a frying pan on a high heat. When the butter starts to sizzle (but don't let it go brown) drop in two tablespoons of the batter. Tip the pan so the batter covers the whole of the base and cook for a couple of minutes. When the underside has cooked, loosen the pancake away from the sides and toss it in the air so it falls back into the pan with the cooked side uppermost. If you feel too nervous about doing this, you can just flip the pancake over with a spatula. Cook for a minute longer and then place the cooked pancake on a warmed plate. Serve with lemon juice and sugar; maple syrup; chocolate sauce and chopped bananas, or your favourite topping.

Mothering Sunday (fourth Sunday after
Lent – UK)

Mothering Sunday, commonly called 'Mother's Day' in the UK and Ireland, falls on the fourth Sunday of Lent (exactly three weeks before Easter Sunday). It is believed to have originated from the sixteenth-century Christian custom of visiting one's mother church every year when mothers would be reunited with their children. Young apprentices and servants were released by their masters that weekend in order to visit their families. The day is now mainly used to celebrate and give thanks for mothers, although it's still recognized in the historical sense by some churches, with attention paid to Mary the mother of Jesus as well as the traditional concept of the Mother Church.

Mother's Day is also celebrated in other countries, although it has no connection with Mothering Sunday. The United States celebrates Mother's Day on the second Sunday in May. It was loosely inspired by the British day and was adopted by social activist Julia Ward Howe after the American Civil War. However, she meant it as a call to unite women against war. In 1870 she wrote the Mother's Day Proclamation.

Hand-painted vase

You will need:

- empty 200 g (7 oz) glass jar
- ribbon
- glass paint, stick-on jewels etc.
- strong glue.

To make

Wash the coffee jar, removing labels and paper from the rim. Dry thoroughly. Decorate the jar with jewels, stickers (glueing if necessary) and/or glass paints. Finish off with a ribbon around the neck of the jar.

Chocolate brownies

A treat for mums everywhere, even if you might have to help your kids make them!

Ingredients (makes 15–20 brownies)

175 g (6 oz) plain chocolate
175 g (6 oz) butter
175 g (6 oz) soft brown sugar
2 eggs, lightly beaten
225 g (8 oz) self-raising flour, sieved.

Method

Preheat oven to 180°C/350°F or 160°C/325°F if fan assisted. Grease a 20 × 20 centimetre (7 × 7 inch) baking tin. In a heavy pan, melt the chocolate and butter over a low heat, stirring occasionally. Stir in the sugar and mix until dissolved. Remove the pan from the heat for a couple of minutes to allow the mixture to cool. Add the beaten eggs and fold in the flour. Pour the mixture into the tin and bake for 15–20 minutes until just firm or a knife comes out clean. Remove from oven and leave to cool on a wire rack for a few minutes. Cut into squares.

Easter (March/April)

While Easter might seem just an excuse to scoff as many Easter eggs as possible, for practising Christians it has a much deeper meaning. It's the time when they commemorate the resurrection of Jesus Christ. On Good Friday, Jesus Christ was crucified. His body was taken down from the Cross, and buried in a cave, and the entrance sealed with a huge stone. On the Sunday, women visiting the grave were shocked to find that the stone had been moved, and the tomb was empty. Jesus himself was seen that day, and for days afterwards by many people. His followers realized that God had raised Jesus from the dead.

Easter falls on a different date every year because the date is based on the old pagan-inspired lunar calendar, rather than our solar one. There are all sorts of activities you can share with your children over the Easter holiday. An Easter egg hunt is a great favourite, where you hide Easter eggs in the garden or house, and the children have to find them. If you want to make the hunt more challenging, write out clues for them to decipher in order to track the eggs down.

Decorating Easter eggs

Encourage your children to think beyond chocolate eggs with these ideas for decorating ordinary hen's eggs, which you don't actually eat, just admire! Before you try any of these techniques, you need to remove the contents of the egg. To do this, first wash and dry the egg. Shake it to break the yolk and then pierce the top and bottom of the egg with a fine needle. Make the hole in the broader end of the egg a little bigger. Hold the egg over a dish and blow through the smaller hole so the contents drop out. When it's completely empty, rest the egg, with the larger hole facing downwards, in an egg carton so it can dry out.

Decorating ideas

Silver foil effects Scrunch up a large square of kitchen foil and then unscrunch it again. Brush the foil on one side with acrylic paint – choose whatever colour you like. Put the egg in the centre of the foil and press the foil against the egg. Make sure you do this gently or you will crack the shell. Remove the egg and let it dry. For an interesting marbled effect use two or three colours, repeating the process as above. Make sure the egg is completely dry before using another colour.

Hand painting Use acrylic paints to create designs on eggs.

Dyeing There are all sorts of natural dyes you can use to change the colour of the egg. For pale red, use beetroot (beets) or raspberries. For light yellow, use orange peel or ground cumin. For a deeper yellow, use ground turmeric. Once you've decided what colour you want your egg, put one or more in a saucepan and cover with cold water. (Use an old saucepan in case you can't get the dye out.) The more eggs you put in, the more dye you'll need. Add a teaspoon of vinegar and your chosen dye and bring the water to the boil. Turn down the heat and simmer for 15 minutes. Remove the eggs and put them in a dish to dry. Wash out the saucepan as soon as you can to get rid of the dye.

Chocolate nests

Ingredients

225 g (8 oz) plain chocolate
50 g (2 oz) butter
2 tablespoons of golden syrup
115 g (4 oz) cornflakes
30 mini eggs.

You will also need:
• paper baking cases
• baking tray
• large saucepan.

Method

Break the chocolate into squares and place in a large saucepan. Add the butter and golden syrup. Stir continuously until the ingredients have melted and blended. Remove the pan from the heat. Add the cornflakes to the mixture and stir thoroughly until they are completely covered in the chocolate mixture. Spoon the cornflake mixture into paper cases. Make a slight hollow in the centre of each 'nest', and put a few eggs in it. Put the tray in a cool place to crisp up. Eat on the same day, which won't be too hard!

Father's Day (June – UK, USA)

Celebrated on different days of the year in different countries, Father's Day was introduced to complement Mother's Day, and has become a significant event in the family calendar. While dads may not want to be fussed over as much as mums, they will still appreciate some extra attention on the day.

Designer T-shirt

Your dad will be very impressed with his own personalized T-shirt.

You will need:

- man's plain white T-shirt
- fabric paint, pens or markers (Berol make a very good range).

To make

First, your children need to decide what they want to put on the T-shirt. They could write a message such as 'The best dad in the world' or 'World's Greatest Dad' or they could draw a picture, based on their dad's favourite hobby or interest, or something abstract. However, it's worth bearing in mind the simplest designs often look the most effective.

If your children are nervous about drawing directly onto the T-shirt, help them to draw the design with a black marker pen onto a sheet of paper. Stick or tape this onto a piece of card and put it inside the T-shirt. The design should show through, and all they have to do is trace over it when they draw their design on the T-shirt.

Iron your T-shirt. Then insert a piece of thin card inside the shirt to prevent the fabric paint going through and staining the back of the T-shirt. You can also draw designs directly onto fabric. In this case use a pencil to draw a faint outline of the design you want to create with the fabric pens, crayons and paints.

If you're using fabric paints, pin or tape your T-shirt to a flat surface to make it easier to draw on. If you're using several colours, makes sure each one dries thoroughly before applying the next one, so the colours don't run into each other. When you've finished your design, leave the T-shirt on a flat surface to dry. Once it's dry, put a clean cotton cloth over the painted area and iron on a hot setting for one to two minutes to set the colour. If you're using fabric crayons, you need to use a cool iron to fix the colours.

Halloween (31 October – All Hallows' Eve)

The event we celebrate today with carved pumpkins and trick-or-treating is a hotchpotch of folklore traditions and ancient beliefs, dating back to Celtic rituals thousands of years ago. Of course today it's a highly commercialized festival for children, with ghostly costumes and sweeties galore. It's the second most popular holiday in the United States, after Christmas. In Mexico, Latin America, and Spain, All Souls' Day, the third day of the three-day Hallowmas observance, is the most important part of the celebration for many people.

Halloween party

You don't have to go to a lot of effort to put on a Halloween party, spending hours draping cobwebs and cut-out bats and witches everywhere. The very fact it's Halloween is enough of a thrill for children, especially after dressing up and going trick-or-treating. Just keep the room dark (replace a couple of light bulbs with red or green ones) and put on some creepy music.

Apple bobbing remains one of the most popular Halloween games. Fill a large bowl with apples and water and invite every child to take a bite out of an apple without using their hands.

Another easy game is to divide children into teams of two and give each a white toilet roll. Each team races to be the first to wrap their mummy in toilet roll. For deliciously horrible fun, get children to identify 'body parts' (actually food). Put various items into bowls, and one by one, pass the bowls around. Each child has to shut their eyes and guess what's in the bowl by touch. Use peeled grapes for eyeballs; cold spaghetti for brains; dried apricots for ears; banana peel for a tongue.

Food can be simple but look scary – it's amazing what you can do with a bottle of tomato sauce. The secret is to give everyday food gruesome names. Sausages with tomato sauce become devil's fingers with congealed blood. Red food colouring added to lemonade becomes vampire fizz.

Pumpkin lanterns

You will need:

- large, well-shaped pumpkin
- sharp knife
- tealight.

To make

Using a sharp knife, cut a round hole in the top of the pumpkin and remove the lid. Using a spoon, scoop out the seeds and flesh. Draw a face on the pumpkin with a biro so you can rub it off easily if you make a mistake. Cut out eyebrows, eyes, nose and mouth, making stabbing movements rather than slicing ones with the knife. Gently scrape away the flesh on the inside of the face until it's only one centimetre thick. Using a teaspoon, scoop out a hollow in the centre of the base of the pumpkin. Place the tealight in this hollow, put the lid back on and place your jack-o'-lantern in the window.

figure 16 pumpkin lantern

Bonfire Night (5 November)

Guy Fawkes night marks the occasion when a group of Catholics, led by Guy Fawkes, angry at the way Catholics were hounded in England, conspired to blow up the Houses of Parliament, the seat of British government, in 1605. The plotters hid barrels of gunpowder in the cellar below the House of Lords but luckily the plot·was foiled. Today, bonfires are lit and fireworks let off in memory of this event. The event is also celebrated in such places as Newfoundland (Canada) and parts of New Zealand.

Toffee apples

Ingredients

8 eating apples
8 toffee apple sticks
225 g (8 oz) demerara sugar
115 ml (4 fl oz) water
$^1/_2$ tsp cider vinegar
1 tbsp golden syrup
30 g (1$^1/_2$ oz) butter.

Method

Wash and dry the apples and insert the sticks into the core of each apple. Line a baking tray with greaseproof paper. Put all the ingredients into a heavy saucepan and stir over a low heat until dissolved. Boil to about 140°C/290°F or until the toffee reaches the 'soft crack' stage or forms 'bendy' strands when dropped into cold water. This can take between ten and 15 minutes. Remove from the heat and cool for a few minutes. Dip each apple into the mixture, making sure all areas of the apple are covered. Stand each apple on the baking tray to set.

Diwali (October/November – Hindu festival)

Celebrated by Hindus and Sikhs, this is the Hindu New Year, lasting for three to five days. The colourful festival of lights commemorates the legend of Prince Rama and Sita's homecoming after the defeat of Ravana (the demon king). It's celebrated with fireworks, lights, food and gifts, and is the largest festival in South Asia.

Candle holder

Diwali is known as the 'festival of lights' because houses, shops, and public places are decorated with small earthenware oil lamps called diyas, lit to help guide the goddess Lakshmi into people's homes.

You will need:

- air-drying clay
- acrylic paint
- flower petals
- PVA glue
- a tealight.

To make

Take some clay and shape it into a small bowl over the bottom of a cup. Leave the clay to dry all over. Add petals with a little PVA (white) glue, and paint the diya all over with glue to give it a shiny finish. Place a tealight inside.

Kheer

An Indian version of rice pudding which is especially popular at Diwali. It can be served warm or chilled.

Ingredients (serves 4)

1/4 cup long grain rice (preferably basmati rice), washed and drained
4–5 cups milk
2 cardamom seeds, crushed
2 tbsp almonds (blanched, slivered)
pinch of saffron threads, soaked in a little hot milk
1 tbsp skinned pistachio nuts (chopped)
1 tbsp raisins (optional)
3–4 tbsp sugar.

Method

Put the rice, milk and cardamom in a saucepan. Bring to the boil and then turn down the heat and simmer gently until the rice is soft and the grains are starting to break up (approximately 60 minutes). Add the almonds, pistachio, saffron and raisins and simmer for three to four minutes. Add the sugar and stir gently until completely dissolved. Remove from heat and allow to cool. Serve warm or chilled.

Thanksgiving (US – November)

Thanksgiving Day is a hugely important family festival celebrated in the US, Canada and several other countries. It has its roots in a feast held by the pilgrim colonists in 1621, a Puritan sect who left England, famously sailing on the *Mayflower*, in search of a better life. The pilgrims were so grateful for such a bountiful harvest, following a very hard winter, that they held a special harvest festival celebration. In 1863 President Lincoln proclaimed Thanksgiving Day and today it's held on the fourth Thursday in November.

The thanksgiving meal generally consists of the traditional turkey, stuffing, mashed potatoes, cranberry sauce and corn but people cook a huge variety of side dishes and puddings too.

Cornbread

You'll see that this recipe and the one below use the US cookery measurements of cups and spoons. These measurements don't convert easily into UK cookery measurements. For accuracy, it's best to use a set of differently sized US cups, which you can get from any good cookery shop.

Ingredients

1 cup plain all-purpose flour
$^1/_2$ cup sugar
4 tsp baking powder
$^3/_4$ tsp salt
1 cup yellow cornmeal
2 eggs
1 cup milk
$^1/_4$ cup shortening (butter).

Method

Heat the oven to 220°C/425°F. Sift together the flour, sugar, baking powder and salt; stir in the cornmeal. Add the eggs, milk, and melted butter. Beat for about a minute until smooth. Pour into a greased 20 × 20 × 5 centimetres (9 × 9 × 2 inch) loaf tin and bake for 20–25 minutes.

Quick pumpkin pie

Ingredients

2 cups puréed pumpkin
2 eggs (beaten)
$^1/_2$ tsp salt
$1^1/_4$ cups brown sugar
400 g (12 oz) can evaporated milk
1 tsp cinnamon
1 tsp nutmeg
$^1/_2$ tsp cinnamon
$^1/_4$ cup butter (melted)
1 unbaked 20 centimetres (9 inch) deep-dish pastry case (or line a deep 20 centimetres/9 in tart tin with shortcrust pastry).

Method

In a large bowl, combine all the ingredients and mix well. Pour the mixture into the pastry case. Bake in a preheated oven at 180°C/350°F for approximately 45 minutes or until set through.

Topping

1 small carton of whipped cream
1/2 cup caster sugar.

Blend all ingredients together and use to top pie.

Hanukkah (Jewish festival – December)

This Jewish festival of lights is held over eight days in December, and remembers the Jews' struggle for religious freedom. Families light one candle on the menorah (special candelabra) for each night of the celebration, ending with eight candles on the last night. People celebrate with food and the exchange of gifts.

Playdough menorah

You will need:

- Playdough (see p. 165)
- large candles
- small candles.

To make

Roll out a piece of playdough and press to form a base. Place a large candle in the middle and four small candles on each side.

Latkes

Ingredients

5 large potatoes
1 onion
5 eggs, beaten
1 tsp salt
freshly ground pepper.

Method

Peel the potatoes and onion and grate them into a large bowl. Crack the eggs into a bowl and add to the potato and onion mixture with some salt and pepper. Use a wooden spoon to mix together.

Pour enough oil into a frying pan to cover the bottom of the pan. Use a large spoon to place spoonfuls of batter into the pan. Fry the latkes for about five minutes on a medium flame. Turn the latkes over and fry for a few more minutes, until brown on both sides. Remove and place on a plate to cool. Serve with apple sauce.

Christmas Day (25 December)

Celebrated all over the world, every country has its own traditions and customs when it comes to celebrating Christmas. The prospect can make children delirious with excitement – and parents delirious with worry about the expense. If you're concerned that blatant commercialism has eclipsed the true meaning of Christmas, try to get your children to appreciate its deeper significance.

Advent calendar

The word 'Advent' comes from the Latin word *Adventus*, which signifies the arrival of Christ. Advent is the beginning of the Church year for most churches in the Western tradition. It begins on the fourth Sunday before Christmas Day, which is the Sunday nearest 30 November, and ends on Christmas Eve on 24 December. Many advent customs involve counting the days until Christmas begins with candles, wreaths or calendars. Why not try helping your children to make their own advent calendar this year?

You will need:

- 2 sheets of coloured card 30 × 40 centimetres (12 × 16 inches)
- pencil
- craft knife
- cutting board
- paper clips
- colouring pencils/paints
- old Christmas cards
- paste
- Blu Tack
- ribbon.

To make

On one of the sheets of paper, draw 25 squares (for the windows) all the same size and one large one in the middle (this is for Christmas Day), leaving a 2 centimetres (³/₄ inch) border around the edge of the paper and making sure that all the windows are evenly spaced. Write the numbers from 1 to 24 on the small windows and 25 on the large one.

Rest the paper on a board to protect surfaces, and using the craft knife, cut out three sides of each window. Carefully open each window, but don't push the flap back too much.

Place the first sheet of paper on top of the second, and secure it at the top and bottom with paper clips. With a pencil, lightly draw around the inside of each window. Remove the paper clips and separate the sheets of paper. Draw a picture inside each of the outlined squares, for example, scenes from the Nativity and objects linked to Christmas such as a sprig of holly, a present or a robin. Alternatively cut out pictures from old Christmas cards, and stick a different one on each square.

Turn the sheet over and paste around the edge, taking care not to get any on the back of the windows. Lay this sheet on the second piece of paper and leave to dry under something heavy such as a paperweight. Close all the windows, securing them with Blu Tack if necessary. Make two holes at the top of your calendar and thread ribbon through to hang it up.

Hogmanay (Scotland – 31 December)

It is hard, if not impossible, to ignore Hogmanay – the Scottish word for New Year's Eve – in Scotland. Houses everywhere are ablaze with lights and just about every town and village in Scotland has some kind of street gathering at 'the bells'. 'First footing', or visiting friends and neighbours with gifts, is a traditional New Year custom. It was thought to bring good luck to the house if at the stroke of midnight, as the New Year begins, or soon after, a tall, dark stranger appeared at the door with a lump of coal for the fire, cake and whisky.

'Auld Lang Syne'

After midnight has struck on New Year's Eve, everyone falls into a huge circle, links crossed arms and roars out this song, originally a poem by Robert Burns, the much loved eighteenth-century Scottish poet. No one has a clue what they're singing usually and very few people realize there's more than one verse, so here it is in its entirety!

Should auld acquaintance be forgot,
And never brought to mind?
Should auld acquaintance be forgot,
And auld lang syne?

CHORUS
For auld lang syne, my dear,
For auld lang syne,
We'll tak a cup of kindness yet,
For auld lang syne!

And surely ye'll be your pint-stowp,
And surely I'll be mine,
And we'll tak a cup o kindness yet,
For auld lang syne!

CHORUS
For auld lang syne, my dear,
For auld lang syne,
We'll tak a cup of kindness yet,
For auld lang syne!

We twa hae run about the braes,
And pou'd the gowans fine,
But we've wander'd monie a weary fit,
Sin auld lang syne.

CHORUS
For auld lang syne, my dear,
For auld lang syne,
We'll tak a cup of kindness yet,
For auld lang syne!

We twa hae paidl'd in the burn
Frae morning sun till dine,
But seas between us braid hae roar'd
Sin auld lang syne.

CHORUS
For auld lang syne, my dear,
For auld lang syne,
We'll tak a cup of kindness yet,
For auld lang syne!

And there's a hand my trusty fiere,
And gie's a hand o thine,
And we'll tak a right guid-willie waught,
For auld lang syne!

CHORUS
For auld lang syne, my dear,
For auld lang syne,
We'll tak a cup of kindness yet,
For auld lang syne!

Glossary

Just in case you're baffled by some of the Scottish words, here's a translation:

auld lang syne – times gone by
be – pay for
braes – hills
braid – broad
burn – stream
dine – dinner time
fiere – friend
fit – foot
gowans – daisies
guid-willie waught – goodwill drink
monie – many
morning sun – noon
paidl't – paddled
pint-stowp – pint tankard
pou'd – pulled
twa – two

Eid-ul-Adha (Dates vary)

This Islamic festival lasting up to five days marks the end of Hajj (the holy pilgrimage to Mecca) and is celebrated by Muslims the world over. It starts with Muslims going to the Mosque for prayers, dressed in their best clothes, and thanking Allah for all the blessings they have received. It's also a time when they visit family and friends as well as offering presents. At Eid it's obligatory to give a set amount of money to charity.

Gulab Jamoon

Ingredients (makes about 65)

225 g (8 oz) condensed milk
225 g (8 oz) margarine (softened)
700 g (1½ lb) plain flour – about 3 cups
½ tsp each ground cinnamon, elaichi (cardamom)

1 pinch ground cloves
oil for frying

Sugar glaze
350 g (12 oz) icing sugar
$1/4$ cup hot water at a time

Method

Mix the condensed milk and margarine with the spices until smooth. Add two cups of flour and mix well. Add the final cup of flour a little at a time. Don't add too much flour as the dough should be soft and not dry and cracking. Knead well and cover with a damp cloth.

Make into balls and then into elongated oval shapes before deep frying on a medium heat. Before frying, keep the dough covered at all times with the damp cloth.

Make the sugar glaze by mixing together half the icing sugar and $1/4$ cup of hot water. Add more water and icing sugar as needed. It's easier to apply the glaze when it's warm.

Dip the gulab jamoon into the glaze and lay out on baking sheets or waxed paper to dry.

Almond pudding

Ingredients
2 tbsp rice
2 cups milk
3 tbsp sugar
$1/4$ cup blanched almonds, sliced
1 tsp green cardamom, crushed
$1/2$ tsp kewra essence
silver or gold foil paper (varak).

Method

Soak the rice in water for a few hours. Drain the water off and grind the rice into a smooth paste. In a non-stick saucepan bring the milk to the boil and then simmer. Over a moderately low heat add the rice, sugar and cardamom and stir constantly until the milk thickens. Remove from heat and add the almonds and kewra essence. Put in a serving bowl and chill. Garnish with silver or gold foil paper (varak) and serve.

Eid-ul-Fitr (end of Ramadan)

This is one of the most important Muslim celebrations of the year, marking the end of Ramadan, the month of fasting where Muslims are forbidden to eat or drink between the hours of sunrise and sunset. It takes place the evening after the new crescent moon is seen in the sky the night before. Special services are held, there are processions in the street and everyone wears new clothes. The highlight is a special celebratory meal where people exchange gifts, sweets and biscuits.

Hanging moon and stars

You will need:

- thin card in black and yellow
- glue
- scissors
- pencil
- black glitter
- glow in the dark glitter
- invisible thread.

To make

Cut crescent moons out of the yellow card and stars out of the black card. Glue black glitter on the outsides of the moons and glue glow-in-the-dark glitter onto the stars so they glow when the lights are out. Cut invisible thread into different lengths. Glue each star and moon to a length of thread, then attach the other end to the ceiling with Blue Tack.

Coconut sweets

Ingredients (8–10 servings)

2½ cups grated fresh coconut
2 cups sugar
1 tbsp ghee (clarified butter)
½ tsp ground cardamom.

Method

Grind the grated coconut in a blender. Place all the ingredients in a saucepan. Cook over a low heat, stirring all the time. When the mixture is sticky and about to scorch the bottom of the pan, remove from the heat. Turn out onto a greased breadboard. Roll out the mixture with a greased rolling pin until 1 centimetre (½ inch) thick. Leave to cool for five minutes. With a sharp knife cut into diamond-shaped pieces.

05

plays and puppet shows

In this chapter you will learn:

- how to put on a play at home
- how to make quick costumes
- how to make simple props
- how to make a puppet theatre and puppets from household objects.

Watch children play together and you'll notice how easily they slip into a world of make believe. They'll make up endless imaginary scenarios and play happily for hours as shopkeepers, teachers, doctors and vets mimicking people and situations they encounter in their everyday life. This type of creative play is an essential part of the development of children, boosting their confidence and self-esteem and helping them gain a better understanding of themselves and others. It also teaches them invaluable social skills, as it necessarily involves taking turns, listening and cooperating. Learning to get on with other people and accepting their differences will stand your child in good stead in later years.

Ways to encourage children to act up

The more you can involve your child in dramatic play, the better – anything from singing a song to putting on a play. As a parent you don't have to have a degree in theatre management to get the ball rolling, just enthusiasm and an ability to suspend your critical judgement. Here are some ideas to inspire your child's imagination:

- Keep a dressing-up box with an assortment of clothes, hats, shoes and accessories – anything that can be turned into a costume (see p. 90).
- Encourage your child to read as much as possible. Share your favourite poems and books with them to fire their imagination. Play storytapes in the car.
- Drama lessons are a great way to bring shy children out of their shell. They don't have to cost a fortune either – find out what's going on locally.
- Encourage your child to act in the school play. They might not land a leading role (it's always someone else's child who gets that) but a walk-on part is just as good. Alternatively, they could help make the scenery or props – there are plenty of off-stage jobs to do.
- Take your child to see interesting, thought-provoking plays (but make sure the content is age-appropriate). See if you can arrange for a backstage tour – the best way for children to find out what's involved in putting on a play professionally.
- Encourage self-expression through singing and dancing. Put on some music and dance with your children. Who cares if you look daft – they will love it and so will you! Introduce

them to different sorts of music; encourage them to learn to play a musical instrument (but don't push it if your child really isn't interested).

• Be a good audience. When your child proudly performs in front of you, resist the urge to criticise or nit-pick. Children thrive on praise, not negativity.

Putting on a play at home

Writing and staging a play is one of the most fun and exhilarating activities children can do at home. It's something the whole family can take part in, even younger children. By about the age of four most children can learn a few easy lines, and can sing and dance and pretend to be other characters. Toddlers can take part as well, with a walk-on role which requires very little dialogue.

Contrary to what you might think, helping your children to put on a play doesn't require expert theatre skills, nor do you have to sit up half the night making elaborate costumes. All you need is enthusiasm, a script, actors, a few props, simple costumes and somewhere to perform the play.

Ideas for plays

Encouraging children to write their own play is a brilliant way to fuel their imagination and improve their literacy skills. Here are some suggestions to get them started:

Fairytales and nursery rhymes are a good starting point, especially if younger children will be taking part. Their familiarity makes them easy to act, plus the costumes are easy to improvise. Older children can have fun giving conventional stories a twist or adding humour. For example, take a well-known character from a book or film and put them in a different setting – Tinkerbell from *Peter Pan* could stomp off in one of her jealous rages when Peter Pan is paying Wendy too much attention and end up in modern day London by mistake. How would she cope? What would she do? How would she get back to Never Never Land?

Improvisation involving individual characters. Give each child a character, a location and an event which they have to act out, for example, Cinderella in a shoe shop trying to find her magic slipper.

Adventure stories. Plays with plenty of action are a good choice for energetic children, especially boys. Plots featuring goodies and baddies give kids lots of opportunities for full-on acting. Get your children to come up with some exciting plot lines. If they're stuck for ideas, they could draw on their favourite heroes and superheroes for inspiration (Robin Hood, Superman), or make their own up. Other scenarios you could suggest include a shipwreck, a spy who's found out, a rescue operation for a dragon in distress (a change from a damsel!), outwitting a thief and so on.

Plays reflecting real life. Encourage children to draw on their own experiences, for example, a school bully who gets his come-uppance; an unpleasant teacher who becomes nice; a lonely child who discovers a talent and makes friends.

How to present a playscript

Scripts for plays are written in a particular format so everyone knows what's going on. Here are some guidelines, but you don't have to follow them slavishly – what you're aiming for is clarity in terms of dialogue and directions.

- Put the title of the play on the first page.

- Acts are usually written with Roman numerals or spelled out: Act II, Act Two. Scenes are usually written with numbers, for example, Scene 3. Begin each act or scene at the top of a new page.

- Put the cast list on the next page, in order of appearance. Include a brief description of each character.

- Describe the setting before the start of each new scene.

- It's useful to have a narrator telling the audience what's going on between scenes, to move the storyline along and introduce characters. The narrator can also act as a prompt if anyone forgets their lines or forgets their cue.

- Write the characters' names in capitals on the left-hand side of the page. Leave a good space and then start speech/stage directions alongside each character. Put characters' names in capitals whenever they appear in the script so they stand out.

- Add stage directions. These are vital as they tell the actors what to do and who else (if anyone) is in the scene. They should be written in the present tense, italicized and put into brackets. Put them before or between the character's lines, so the actor knows what to do, for example:

PRINCESS STROPPY (*stamping her foot*) I won't wear that stupid dress! I hate dresses. (*She throws the dress into the river and storms off.*)

Below is an example of a playscript, which shows you how to lay it out. The play is for seven main players (four children and three pixies) and a narrator but you could adapt it for more or less children. For example, you could have two children, just one pixie and an adult playing the parent. The narrator could also be a parent. The plot's very simple – three pixies keep stealing toys from careless children, but when they steal Angela's teddy they get more than they bargained for, as Angela and her new friends, John, Sally and Mark, set a trap for the pixies and find out exactly what they've been doing. The pixies are very angry at being found out, but it turns out that they steal toys because they are jealous. No one has ever given them toys. The children take pity on the pixies and promise to let them come and play with their toys whenever they want. But they must promise to give back all the toys they've stolen and to never do it again. The repentant pixies agree.

THE TOY SNATCHERS

A play in three acts by the Brown family

Cast (in order of appearance)
Narrator
Angela
Mother of Angela
John
Sally
Mark
Mischief – assistant pixie
Teaser – head pixie
Trouble – assistant pixie

Act I, Scene 1

A summer's afternoon in the park. Three children – two boys and a girl – are playing ball. A little girl, ANGELA, is sitting on a park bench with her MOTHER, who's having a long conversation on her mobile phone, gossiping to a friend. The MOTHER is saying things like 'No! She didn't!' and 'I don't believe it' in incredulous tones.

ANGELA is lonely as she and her parents have just moved to this town and she doesn't know anyone. She's about ten years old, with long hair and is wearing jeans and a jumper. She's hugging a teddy bear close to her. The three children playing ball are JOHN, aged 12, his brother MARK, aged 10, and their sister SALLY, aged 8. They are dressed in jeans and jumpers.

NARRATOR   Once upon a time there was a much loved teddy bear called Boo, who lived with a little girl called Angela. Angela was very lonely because she didn't have any friends.

ANGELA   Oh Boo, (*kissing bear*) I love you so much. You're the best bear in all the world. I don't know what I'd do if I lost you 'cos you're my only friend. I wish I had friends. It's so lonely being on your own. (*Suddenly the children's ball hits her on the arm.*) Ow! (*exclaiming and rubbing her arm*) That hurt! (*The three children come running up to her, full of concern.*)

JOHN   We're so sorry, we didn't mean to hit you. It's just that SALLY here (*pointing to his sister*) is such a rotten shot.

SALLY   (*Indignantly*) No I'm not. It's just that you've got butterfingers and didn't catch the ball. (*She looks concerned*) But we are very sorry.

MARK   To make up for it, would you like to play a game with us? That way there's less chance of you being hit. Oh, by the way, I'm Mark, and this is my sister Sally and my brother John. (*He points to the other two children standing next to him.*)

ANGELA   (*Smiling*) I'm OK and yes I would like to play with you. We've just moved here and I don't know anyone.

JOHN   (*Smiling back*) Oh you'll soon make friends. I mean you've met us, so that's three friends you've got already.

SALLY   And I don't have many people to play with – just my pesky brothers! (*All the children laugh. ANGELA jumps up and joins in the game. She leaves her bear on the park bench next to her mother. The four children start playing catch further away. They are so absorbed in their game and ANGELA'S MOTHER is so busy talking on her mobile, they don't notice a small creature dressed in green with a pointed hat creep from behind the bench, snatch the bear and run off*).

ANGELA   Gosh it's hot (*wiping her brow*). I'll just get some water for us from Mum. (*She runs up to her mother, who is still talking into her mobile phone. ANGELA rummages through a rucksack and gets out a bottle of water. She glances next to it and looks horrified as she sees her bear has gone.*) My bear has gone! (*shouting*) Someone has taken my bear!

The other children come running up, and ANGELA'S MOTHER actually stops talking on the phone.

MARK   Don't worry Angela, we'll find your missing bear. (*ANGELA bursts into tears and they all run off stage to look for the bear. ANGELA'S MOTHER follows, still talking on her mobile phone.*)

Act I, Scene 2

A dimly lit room full of children's toys. A group of pixies, dressed in green and brown with pointed hats, sit around laughing.

TEASER   (*Rubbing his hands together*) That was a good day's work – well done Mischief and Trouble. Look at all the toys we've managed to steal from careless children.

TROUBLE   (*Giggling unkindly*) If they don't look after their toys properly they don't deserve to have them. If I had toys I'd never let them out of my sight, especially teddy bears. (*He picks up a bear and cuddles it. The other pixies nod in agreement.*)

MISCHIEF   (*Holding up ANGELA's bear*) Look at this beautiful bear I found sitting on a bench. You'd think the owner would take better care of him, but she was so busy enjoying herself she didn't notice he'd gone for ages. That was probably my easiest mission ever.

TEASER   (*Frowning*) Okay, now back to business. Our next mission is a pretty big one… A good haul of toys here – four bikes and a scooter left in gardens, six footballs left in the park and goodness knows how many soft toys left on trains and buses… Think of all those poor, sad children sobbing into their pillows tonight… (*The three pixies start laughing again.*)

Act I, Scene 3

ANGELA is back in the park with JOHN, MARK and SALLY. She looks very miserable, and is dabbing her eyes with a handkerchief.

ANGELA   I can't believe my bear has gone! Why would anyone want to take him? We've looked everywhere and he's just vanished into thin air.

SALLY   (*Putting her arm round ANGELA*) Don't worry, we'll find him for you. We're very good at finding missing things.

MARK   (*Frowning*) There's something fishy going on here. At breakfast Mum and Dad were talking about all these toys that keep disappearing all over town. The police are completely baffled.

JOHN (*Looking thoughtful*) I have an idea. Why don't we try and find out who's doing this by setting a trap. We could put Sally's bear on that bench, hide and see if anyone comes along to take it.

ANGELA (*Looking excited*) That's a great idea.

MARK Fantastic plan! Let's go and hide over there behind that bush.

The four children quickly go and hide behind a bush. After a short while, a small, green figure runs onto the stage, grabs the bear from the bench and runs off again into the wings. The children run out of their hiding place, shouting, 'Stop thief!' and chase after the pixie into the wings.

Act II

Back in the pixie cave. The children's chase has led them here. They are standing together, looking in astonishment at a huge heap of toys. The pixie who ran off with the bear is nowhere to be seen.

JOHN I don't believe it – just look at all these toys! There must be hundreds here!

MARK Look, there's my football signed by the team! (*He picks up a football from the pile and looks delighted.*)

SALLY (*Seizing a doll from the heap of toys*) And here's my doll that Granny gave me!

ANGELA (*Darting forward towards the toys*) And look, here's Boo. (*She picks up the bear and cuddles it. SALLY, MARK and JOHN start searching through the heap and discover more toys they or their friends have lost. They're so absorbed in what they're doing they don't notice the three pixies standing in the shadows. The pixies are whispering angrily to themselves.*)

MISCHIEF Well, I say we tie them up and dump them in the blackest, darkest cave we can find or else they'll just carry on poking their horrible fat noses into our business.

TROUBLE I agree! They don't deserve to have their toys back when they didn't look after them properly.

TEASER (*Frowning*) We need to think about this. I mean, look how happy they are to find their toys again. (*He stares at the children, exclaiming with happiness as they find yet more long-lost toys.*)

MISCHIEF   (*Rudely*) There's nothing to think about. Come on! (*He leaps out of the shadows and pounces on JOHN. TROUBLE rushes out too and grabs MARK. The two boys tussle with the two pixies, while ANGELA, SALLY and TEASER look on in horror.*)

ANGELA   (*Screaming*) Stop it, all of you! Stop it right now! (*The boys and pixies break apart and stand glaring at each other and breathing heavily.*)

TEASER   Mischief! Trouble! Come and stand here. (*Looking sulky, the pixies obey and go and stand next to TEASER.*) I'm ashamed of you two – you know the rules. No contact *ever* with human children and that includes fighting. Do you hear me?

MISCHIEF & TROUBLE   Yes, we hear you. And we're sorry.

ANGELA   (*Approaching them*) But why do you do it? Why do you steal all our toys? We never did any harm to you.

TEASER   (*Looking sorry*) It's just that we never had any toys of our own when we were children. And when we saw how careless you human children are with your toys, leaving them all over the place and forgetting about them, we thought we'd teach you a lesson and have the toys for ourselves.

SALLY   Never had any toys of your own? But that's awful.

ANGELA   (*Stepping forward and handing her bear to MISCHIEF*) You have my bear. He's called Boo. I love him very much but I think you need him more than me.

MISCHIEF   (*Astonished*) You're giving me your bear? But why should you do that when I've been so horrid to you? (*He looks on the verge of tears*) I don't deserve it.

SALLY   (*Putting an arm round the pixie*) You haven't been very nice but now we know why you took all those toys we forgive you.

JOHN   (*Brightening up*) I've just had another great idea. If you stop taking children's toys, you can come and play with our toys whenever you like.

TEASER   (*Clapping his hands*) Oh, that's wonderful! Mischief and Trouble, what do you think?

MISCHIEF   We think it's the best idea we've ever heard. (*TROUBLE nods vigorously*) So can we come and play with your toys now?

ALL THE
CHILDREN   Of course!

The three pixies and four children link arms and walk off stage,
chatting and laughing together.

THE END

Props and costumes

A few props and simple costumes will make all the difference to
your children's play. Some plays will need hardly anything, for
instance, *The Toy Snatchers*, our playscript above, is set in the
present day, so actors can just wear their ordinary clothes. The
pixies can wear white leggings and T-shirts, and could wear
green face paint to make them look other-worldly. However,
always make sure that any make-up you use is safe to use on
children, as their skin can be much more sensitive than that of
adults. (Visit the US government's website **www.cfsan.fda.gov**
for more information on additives in products.)

You'll find your children will have plenty of ideas of their own
when it comes to deciding on props and costumes, so be sure to
include them in the process – it's all part of the enjoyment and
will give them great satisfaction.

Ideas for easy costumes

With a little bit of imagination you can make all sorts of
costumes surprisingly quickly. If you're not into sewing, you can
use a glue gun, glue stick, bulldog clip, stapler, fabric glue or
masking tape to hold clothes together or attach fake fur,
sequins, fringes and other items. However, while a glue stick is
fine for attaching paper decorations and sequins to costumes,
you'll need stronger glue for sticking construction paper
together.

If you want to paint on to materials, it's best to use acrylic paint
because it's water-based but waterproof once it dries, is more
durable and gives a more professional look than other paints.
However, there's no reason why you can't use poster paints. Just
remember they're not waterproof.

Keep a stock of black and white bin bags for last-minute
costumes, and don't forget that essential standby, Velcro™,
which can be glued to fabric for easy fastenings. The costumes

don't have to look like something out of a Hollywood extravaganza, but should just represent the character.

> **Safety note**
> Always supervise your children if they're using a glue gun. This is a very handy gadget when it comes to making costumes as it's strong and dries very quickly, but you can easily burn your fingers due to the solvent in it.

Scour charity shops and thrift stores for cheap clothes and accessories. Beg and borrow stuff from friends; buy cheap remnants in sales. Out-grown and out-worn children's clothes can also be adapted.

Common characters

Black cat To black leggings and a black long-sleeved top, add a black tail. To make this, take an old pair of black tights and stuff one leg with scrunched-up newspaper. To attach the tail, pass the other leg around your waist behind you and tie it to the top of the tail. Make cat's ears from black felt and glue on to a black Alice band; draw whiskers and nose on to the face with face paint.

Dog To black leggings, add a black hooded sweatshirt, dog's collar and lead; for floppy ears, pin a black sock on either side of the hood; for paws, put black socks on hands and feet. Draw a black nose and whiskers on the face with face paint. Carry a ball or squeaky toy.

Harry Potter Add a black cape, a pair of round glasses, a broomstick and draw a lightning scar on the forehead. Owl optional! (If you want to add a wizard's hat see p. 94.)

Cowboy Checked shirt, waistcoat, jeans, boots, cowboy hat, neckerchief, belt, holster and toy gun.

Princess Long floaty, glitzy dress.

Fairy White leotard and leggings/tights, worn with a skirt made from an old net curtain. The curtain should already be gathered so you just need to fasten the skirt with staples or stitches. Make a wand by cutting a star shape out of thick cardboard, and covering it with silver foil. Make the stick part with a dowel, or roll up card or paper into a tube, glue the ends, and cover with silver foil.

To make fairy wings fast!

Take two wire coat hangers and pull each one out to make a wing shape. Make sure that both 'wings' look the same. Untwist hooks of hangers and then join hangers by twisting wire together. Cover with masking tape. Cover wings with any gauzy or stretchy fabric. Alternatively, cut the legs off a pair of white tights and pull them over each wing, stretching them tight but taking care not to snag them. Tie ends around the twisted wires. Glue on glitter around the edges of the wings. Tie ribbons to middle of wings, bring ribbons over shoulders, cross in front and tie round waist at back.

Pirate Over-sized baggy shorts or cut-off and frayed jeans; stripy top or billowy white shirt tucked in; wide belt or rope; eyepatch; clip-on gold earring; bandana worn around head and tied at the back. Add moustache and stubble with face paints. Finish off with toy parrot attached to the shoulder with craft wire.

Clown Over-sized shirt and trousers, held up with braces; pork pie hat and clown make-up (white face and red lips). Oh, and don't forget the red nose!

Gypsy Long patterned skirt; peasant top; shawl; head scarf; lots of jewellery such as bracelets, beads, necklaces and earrings.

Fairytale characters For characters such as Alice in Wonderland and Goldilocks, put a white apron with a bib over a blue dress. Add white socks, shoes and a blue Alice band. Coloured tights and tunics made from squares of material tied at the side come in handy for all sort of boys' costumes from Robin Hood to fantasy characters.

Princes and soldiers An old white pillowcase transforms into a tunic or tabard. Make openings for head and arms by cutting slits in the closed end and sides of pillowcase. Paint symbols on front of tunic with fabric paint (for example, St. George's Cross); even a chain mail pattern if you're feeling very creative. Put a thick leather belt around the waist and add leggings or tights worn with boots.

Halloween costumes

Dracula Add a black cape to black trousers, white shirt, bow tie and black shoes. Slick hair back with gel, attach fangs to teeth and a spot or two of fake blood (be careful as it can stain).

Ghost A white sheet makes an excellent ghost. Cut two holes for the eyes and gather material around the neck, fixing with safety pins.

Mummy Wind a white, stretchy bandage around arms, legs, torso, and face. Or add a gruesome face mask if a head bandage is too suffocating.

Witch A long black skirt, black leggings, black boots/shoes. What brings this costume alive is a big black cloak. Make one super fast by taking a large square piece of black fabric. Tear the edges to make it look suitably witchy. Cut a hole in the middle, large enough for a child to put his or her head through and you have a cloak. Finish the look with a witch's hat. Buy one or make your own (see below).

Dressing-up box

Keep a box full of old clothes and accessories for plays and dressing up. Look out for things you can add to the box at second-hand stores and charity shops/thrift stores such as boleros and anything in a floaty fabric. Useful items worth hoarding include:

- old evening dresses; glitzy tops; feather boas; petticoats
- furry gloves; fur fabric remnants – handy for animal costumes
- men's shirts – white or plain collarless ones are especially useful as they go with any type of costume.
- old curtains for capes; old net curtains for princess and fairy costumes.
- jewellery – necklaces, bracelets, brooches (good for fastening cloaks and capes)
- bulldog clips to fasten clothes
- belts – all types; different colours, fabrics and sizes;
- curtain tiebacks – ones with tassels on
- scarves, shawls, old aprons
- old hats – berets, flat caps, cowboy hats, tea cosy for sultan's hat
- fabric remnants.

Making hats

You can make hats really easily starting with a basic hat band, made from stiff paper, which you can buy in different colours. Measure around your child's head, allowing for an extra 3 centimetres (1 inch) to fasten it and cut the band to fit. Staple or glue the ends together. From this basic idea you can make a number of different hats.

Indian headdress Glue feathers to the band.

Crown Using a band about 10 centimetres (4 inches) wide, cut triangles or squares out of the top and decorate with fake jewels, beads, glitter etc.

Cone hat The basis for witches' and wizards' hats. Fold a 30 × 60 centimetres (12 × 24 inches) sheet of newspaper in half lengthways. Cut out a quarter circle and open the paper into a half circle. Roll the half circle into a cone to fit the head. Tape or staple the cone together, neatening up the edges. You now need to add a brim. Put the cone on a sheet of stiff paper and draw around it. Draw a larger circle around the first circle and cut it out Draw five tabs inside the inner circle. Cut out the inner circle around the tabs. Fold the tabs back. Slip the brim over the cone and glue or tape the tabs to the cone.

Ideas for easy props

A play isn't complete without props. Putting on a play at home gives you access to all sorts of items you can use on stage. Furniture is especially useful. For instance, in *The Toy Snatchers*, the living room sofa can be turned into a park bench and a table turned on its side with a sheet thrown over it becomes the pixies' cave. The children's own toys can also be put to good use. Soft toys can be used to represent animals; wands and witches' hats turn actors into magicians; crowns and tiaras make kings, queens, princes and princesses.

Kitchen utensils make excellent props. A colander can double as a helmet; a teapot as Aladdin's lamp. Other useful props include plastic cutlery and plates, old mobile phones, old keys, baskets (good for fairy tales such as *Little Red Riding Hood*), an outdoor broom (useful in fairy tales like *Cinderella*, or can double as a witch's broom).

Inflatable swimming pool toys make excellent props for plays involving water – use a blow-up shark, dolphin and boat, for instance, and you almost have an instant play.

Throws, rugs and old curtains make excellent props. Blue silky fabric thrown on the floor can become water; a brown fleecy throw can become an animal costume; green fabric on the floor can become grass.

Boxes make incredibly useful props. They can be stacked and rearranged in many different ways. For landscaping they can make very good cities, rocks and caves. That's not mentioning their use as costumes; small boxes are great for robot heads and large cardboard boxes (the kind that white goods are packed in) make excellent houses, cars, buses, boats, stagecoaches – the list is endless.

Empty mineral bottles can be turned into an oxygen pack for an astronaut by taping the bottles together, adding a length of plastic tubing and spray painting with silver paint.

Dick Whittington's cat

A quick and easy way to make props is with newspaper and masking tape. Take a large sheet of newspaper and scrunch it into the shape you want. Bind masking tape around the shape and finish off by painting. Try this technique out for Dick Whittington's Cat!

Make the main body by scrunching up newspaper and winding masking tape around the shape. For the head, scrunch up newspaper into a ball. Wrap masking tape around the paper, making sure it keeps its shape as a head. To make the legs, roll the newspaper into two long tubes, starting at the corner. Wind the masking tape around, taking care not to leave any gaps. Cut the tubes in half and you have four 'legs'. For the tail, roll up newspaper again, starting from the corner and wind masking tape around the length. Tape the parts to the body with the masking tape and paint with black acrylic paint. For whiskers, cut two drinking straws into eight lengths and tape on to the front of the head. When the paint is dry, paint on a white nose and eyes.

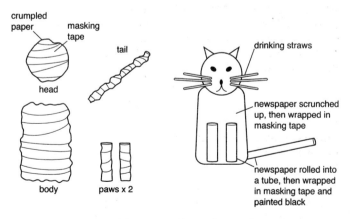

figure 17 newspaper and masking tape can make a very good cat

Pirate sword

Using thick card, cut out the shape of a sword. Make the handle with crumpled newspaper bound with masking tape. Cover the sword part with silver foil and paint the handle with black acrylic paint.

figure 18 pirate sword

Putting on a puppet show

There's something magical about puppets and the way children respond to them. Helping them put on a puppet show will provide endless hours of excitement for children of all ages.

To make a puppet theatre

You can make an impressive puppet theatre from a large cardboard box (far cheaper and more interesting than buying a ready-made one). Ask at your local DIY store for a box – they should have plenty this size. As you need to use a sharp knife when cutting portions out, make sure you supervise children at all times.

You will need:

- strong cardboard box
- craft knife
- fabric for curtain
- curtain wire with hooks
- scenery.

To make

Remove flaps from the box – this will be the back of the theatre. Using a craft knife, cut a large rectangle out of the front of the box. Cut out the 'floor' out of the box. Paint the box using poster or acrylic paints and allow them to dry. To make scenery, take two or three pieces of fabric (felt or calico are good choices) and cut to fit the back of the box. Draw a scene directly onto each piece of fabric or stick on pictures from a magazine. Make a channel at the top of each piece of fabric by folding over 3 centimetres (1 inch) and gluing into place. Thread a bamboo stick through each channel, so it protrudes 5 centimetres (2 inches) either side of the board. To use your scenery board, drop it down at the back of the theatre so the ends of the bamboo rest on the sides.

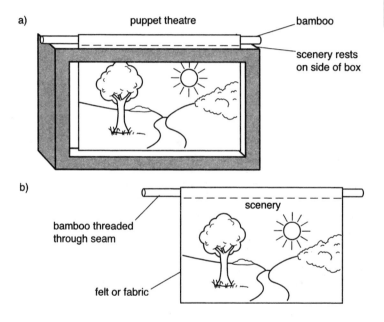

a)

puppet theatre   bamboo

scenery rests on side of box

b)

bamboo threaded through seam

scenery

felt or fabric

figure 19 a simple box can make an impressive puppet theatre

Make curtains out of red velvet remnants. Each curtain needs to be the same width as the theatre, to allow for gathering. Make a heading at the top of each curtain by folding 3 centimetres (1 inch) of fabric over and stitching or gluing the edge in place, leaving a channel. Thread curtain wire through the headings of both curtain. Attach a curtain hook either side of the theatre, on the inside. Attach curtain wire with curtains to these hooks.

Making puppets

You can make puppets out of virtually anything – card, yoghurt pots, socks, gloves. Cut pictures out of magazines or comics and stick them on to card, or cut out faces from family photos to stick onto card. Use lollysticks, craft sticks or dowel to support the puppets.

Finger puppets

Roll cardboard into a tube small enough to fit on your children's fingers. Make separate heads out of card – for the animals below, copy the shapes onto card and cut out. For the cow, use white card, draw on eyes and nose and paint on large black spots. For the frog, draw eyes and mouth as shown and stick on a scrap of red felt for the tongue. Stick on feet. For the horse, make the mane with scraps of felt or wool. Add little felt ears and draw on eyes and nose.

figure 20a finger puppets

Wooden spoon puppets

It's very easy to transform wooden spoons into engaging puppets by simply drawing faces on them with permanent black felt-tip markers. For human faces you can glue on scraps of wool for hair or add little hats made from felt. It's the same principle for animal faces. Draw on the features and add ears, a mane or whiskers etc. from scraps of felt.

Shadow puppets

Cut cardboard into appropriate shapes (see figure 20c). Remember you're drawing characters in profile so choose ones with strong features. They don't have to be solid shapes so you

figure 20b wooden spoon puppet

figure 20c shadow puppets need characters with strong features

can cut holes in them for eyes etc. as the light will shine through them. Glue on to lollysticks, wooden kebab sticks or chopsticks. For the show, project a strong light from a lamp or torch at an angle onto the puppets and onto a plain wall. The angle of the light will make the puppets appear larger.

Glove puppet

Use a glove to make a glove puppet – it's that easy. The thumb and little finger are the arms, and the middle three fingers represent the body and head. Your children can have fun transforming gloves into all sorts of characters. Cut a circle of card about the size of the middle three fingers, draw on a face or stick on a face cut from a magazine. Stick the 'head' onto the glove and attach strands of wool for hair. Make clothes for the body out of scraps of felt.

figure 20d gloves make perfect puppets

Sock puppet

You will need:

- thick socks
- black felt-tip pen.

To make

Socks make great hand puppets – pop one on to your hand as if you're wearing a mitten, with the heel part facing backwards. Push the toe part in between your thumb and other fingers and you have an instant face with a mouth which you can turn into any weird and wonderful creature. Children can use their imagination to create a family of sock puppets.

To make a dragon sock puppet, take a red or green sock, glue green felt spines onto the leg part (try the sock on your hand to determine the right position), and stick on dots for eyes, or you can buy 'wobbly' eyes from craft shops.

Go on, have a go! Be creative!

figure 20e dragon sock puppet

06

special family gatherings

In this chapter you will learn:
• games to break the ice
• team games for all ages
• old favourites such as bingo, charades and tiddlywinks
• games for the garden, including golf and skittles.

Games and activities make great ice-breakers when you're bringing together a mix of relations who might not know each other very well. Keep in mind the age range of the people who'll be present at whatever event you're planning and choose the games accordingly. It goes without saying that very boisterous activities enjoyed by younger members of the family aren't going to be as popular with elderly relations with hip problems. Also allow for breaks between games or people will leave exhausted!

Four good icebreakers

Passing the orange

Players try to pass an orange down the line using their chin. Players divide into teams and stand in a line next to their leaders. Each leader is given an orange which is tucked between chin and chest. On the word 'go' the leaders have to pass the orange to the person next to them, without using their hands. The orange is then passed from one player to the next. If anyone drops the orange, it goes back to the leader and you have to start again. The first team to successfully pass the orange down the line wins.

Hello circle

People can't fail to get to know each other in this greetings game. You all stand in a large circle, facing inwards, including the person chosen as leader. The leader shakes hands with the person on his or her right, saying 'Hello' and the neighbour says 'Hello' back. The leader then greets the next person in the same way, going round the whole circle. The second person, who was on the leader's right, follows and shakes hands with everyone in turn and says 'Hello'. Behind the second follows the third player, and so on.

In this way the ring slowly turns in on itself, and everyone greets everyone else. Players nearest the leader at the start will have to walk the farthest to pass around the circle, and the last player of all – who started on the leader's left – doesn't need to move, as everyone, sooner or later, will pass in front.

Cat and dog

A very silly game where two objects representing a cat and dog are passed around a circle, accompanied by set questions and answers. You can use any household item for the cat and dog – the more ridiculous the better – but make sure they don't have any sharp edges.

How to play

You all sit in a circle. The first player passes, say, a wooden spoon to the player on the right, saying 'I found this dog'. 'This what?' the player asks. 'This dog,' repeats the first player. The second player passes the spoon to the third player saying 'I found this dog'. 'This what?' they have to respond. The second player turns back to the first and asks 'This what?', 'This dog,' says the first player. 'This dog,' says the second player to the third player. The third player turns to the fourth player, and the same routine has to be repeated. When a new player receives the spoon, they must ask 'This what?' The players then have to send the question back along the line to the first player and the answer has to be passed up by every player in between them.

Once everyone has got the hang of this, the first player says that a cat is going to take part in the game. The cat can be, say, a tea towel. Both objects are started off at the same time, the wooden spoon (the dog) to the left and the tea towel (the cat) to the right. It gets hilarious when the two animals pass each other halfway round the circle, so players have to answer questions about the dog and the cat from both directions.

Beetle

This is a hectic version of the classic Beetle Drive. Players pair up and each pair has a sheet of paper, a pen, a dice and shaker. The aim is to draw a full beetle. Someone shouts 'Go' and each

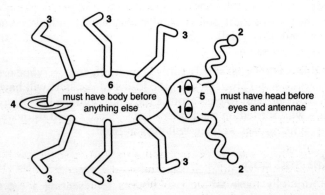

figure 21 a completed beetle

pair simultaneously starts trying to throw a six. Each couple must take turns in throwing and the speed and crazy competitiveness adds to the fun. When a six is thrown, the thrower draws an oval body. Now that couple can add a tail when they throw a four, and a leg each time they throw a three. When they throw a five, they can add a head. Only then can they add feelers (two twos) and eyes (two ones). As soon as any couple has drawn a complete beetle, they shout 'Beetle' and each pair adds up their score. (A full beetle tots up to 39.)

Team games for all ages

Prodding the pig

Each team needs one long, thin balloon and a walking stick or long umbrella. Teams stand at the starting line, with the finish line 3–4.5 metres (10–15 feet) away. The first player rests his balloon (or pig) on the starting line and holds the stick or umbrella. Everyone has to start with their pig in exactly the same place or they can gain an unfair advantage. Someone shouts 'Go!' and players have to push their 'pigs' over the end line and then push them back to the start. (You can only prod your pig at either end of the balloon.) The next player takes over and so on, until all team members have had a go. The first team to finish wins.

Fanning the kipper

Each player is given a folded newspaper and a 'kipper' cut out of a piece of tissue paper (any fish shape will do). Each player has to make his or her kipper move from the start to the finish line by fanning it with the newspaper. The first player to get the kipper to the end wins. This can also be played in a relay fashion in two teams.

Waiter, hurry up!

The aim of this team game is to race through your line while keeping a table tennis ball balanced on a plate. It's a good indoor party game as you don't need a lot of space, but make sure you clear the room of any obstacles first.

Players divide into two teams and appoint two captains. Each team lines up behind their captain, who is given a paper plate with a table tennis ball on it. Whoever is supervising the game shouts 'Go!' and then the captain, holding the plate and ball, faces the other team members and attempts to weave in and out of the line without dropping the plate or ball. If a teammate drops the plate or ball, it's back to the beginning again!

When you reach the end of the line, you rush back to the top and hand the plate and ball to the next team member, saying, 'Here is your breakfast, Sir (or Madam).' You then run back to the end of the line, and the next player, as the waiter, holding the ball on the plate, weaves in and out of the line. Play carries on this way until every team member has been the waiter. The first team to finish wins.

Pack it in!

For this game you need two suitcases packed with old clothes. One suitcase should contain clothes and items for a male, the other clothes and items for a female. (For male items you could include hats, silly glasses, false noses, fake beards and moustaches, wigs etc.; for female items you could have lipstick, wigs, jewellery, scarves etc. – anything that can be used by the players.)

The male players form one team; the female players form the other. Place both cases a reasonable distance away from the players. On the word 'Go!' the first players hop to the suitcases. The female player hops to the male suitcase, puts on the clothes and uses any items there as well. The male player hops to the female suitcase and does the same. Both players then pick up their suitcase and hop back to the starting line where they put the clothes and items back in the suitcase. Holding the cases and hopping, they put them back where they were and hop back to the start. The next player does exactly the same thing. The first team to finish wins.

Old favourites

Charades

You'll know this entertaining and hilarious game where players take it in turns to act out a word which the other players have to guess. You're not allowed to speak but have to rely on mime and your team's sharp guesswork. It's perfect for a family gathering as everyone knows it and if younger children are a little shy about standing in front of an audience, they can always team up with someone else. It's worth running through the rules before you start as there are lots of different versions of charades. You can also decide on the categories you want to pick words from, for example, you could just have film titles or, narrowing it down even further, titles of horror films.

How to play

The players divide into two teams. Someone who is not playing whispers an idea to act out to the first player. That player begins by miming to the audience if it's a book, a play, a film or a TV programme (or any other categories you have decided to include). If it's a book you unfold your hands as if opening a book; if it's a play you mime curtains drawing back; if it's a film you pretend to roll a movie camera; if it's a TV programme you draw a box in the air. You then tell your team how many words are in the title by holding up the requisite number of fingers. If it's just one word, you tell them how many syllables are in the word by laying the number of fingers on your arm, so if there are two syllables in the word, you lay two fingers on your arm. You then begin miming the word, remembering that you're not allowed to speak.

Other clues you can give your team

If you are miming a title with more than one word in it, you can tell your team which word you're about to mime by holding up the number of fingers again (for example, if you're about to act the third word in your title, you hold up three fingers). To tell your team how many syllables are in the word, lay the number of fingers on your arm, as before. To let your team know which syllable you're about to act out, lay the number of fingers on your arm again.

To show the length of the word, make a 'little' or 'big' sign with your hands outstretched as if you were measuring the width of something.

For the whole word or phrase, draw an imaginary large circle with your hands, starting at the top with both hands touching and ending at the bottom with both hands touching.

'On the nose' (i.e. where someone has guessed correctly): put your finger on your nose, and with the other hand point to the person who made the right guess.

'Sounds like' or 'rhymes with': cup a hand behind your ear as if you're listening to something.

'Longer version of': with your hands, pretend to stretch something.

'Shorter version of': move your hand downwards in a slicing action.

'Plural': link your little fingers together.

'Proper name': tap the top of your head with your hand face down.

'Past tense': wave your hand over your shoulder towards your back.

A letter: move your hand in a chopping motion towards your arm (at the top of your forearm if the letter is near the beginning of the alphabet, the middle of your arm if it's in the middle, and near your wrist if the letter is towards the end of the alphabet).

Once your team has guessed your word, the other team is given a word to act out.

Bingo

A perennial favourite and it's not surprising why as it's really easy to play – you just mark off numbers as they're called out. You can buy bingo sets, which include everything you need to play the game; download bingo cards for free from the internet and laminate them so you can use them over and over; or even make your own – something you and your children could do together.

How to call

The most important person in bingo is the caller. They won't actually be playing bingo, but calling out the all-important numbers between 1 and 90. In the UK, the caller traditionally says something humorous about the numbers as he or she calls them.

Here are the most common nicknames for the single numbers.

Calling single numbers

The caller calls out 'On its own' with single numbers. For example, if 4 comes up, the caller says 'On its own, knock on the door, number 4.'

1 Kelly's Eye; Bingo baby; At the beginning.
2 One little duck; Me and you; Doctor Who.
3 I'm free; One little flea; Debbie McGee.
4 Knock on the door; The one next door.
5 Man alive.

6 Chopsticks.
7 Lucky for some; Lucky; One little crutch.
8 One fat lady; Garden gate.
9 Doctor's orders.

Calling double numbers

When double numbers are the same, the caller says 'All the...' before the nickname and number. So, if the caller is about to call 66 he or she would say, 'All the sixes, clickety-click, 66' or to call 55, he would say, 'All the fives, snakes alive, 55'.

11 Legs eleven.
22 Two little ducks dinky doo.
33 All the feathers; Two little fleas; All the trees, Sherwood Forest.
44 Droopy drawers.
55 Snakes alive.
66 Clickety-click.
77 Sunset strip (from an old TV show).
88 Two fat ladies. (Crowd may answer by shouting 'wobble, wobble'.)

How to play

Everyone has a bingo card which consists of rows of numbers. Once a number is called, you check your card to see if it's there. If it is, you mark it off. If you manage to mark off all the numbers in a single row across the card, that's a line. If you mark off two lines on the same card, that's two lines. If you succeed in marking off all the numbers on your card you shout 'Full house!'

Newmarket (2–6 players)

Also known as Boodle or Stops in the US, Newmarket can be played for fun, as a betting game, or a mixture of the two. You need two packs of cards and matches or counters.

How to play

Use one pack of cards and remove the Ace of Spades, King of Diamonds, Queen of Hearts and Jack of Clubs from another pack. These are the 'horses' the players bet on in the game, and the cards are placed face up in a square on the table. The players start with an agreed number of matches and, before the cards are dealt, each player puts one or more matches on one of the horses. The aim of the game is to have no cards left at the end of the game, and the player holding one of the horses in his hand must try to play it to win the matches on that card.

The cards are dealt to all the players, face down, plus one extra or dummy hand. The player on the left of the dealer starts, and you play any card you want, as long as it's the lowest you have in a suit. The next player must then play a higher card of the same suit, and the game continues in this way until no one can go anymore, or if the Ace is reached. A card you can't follow is called a stop card. This will happen as some of the cards will be in the dummy hand.

When play stops the last player continues with the lowest card he has in suit. During play, anyone who plays a card which matches one of the horses takes all the matches on that card. Once a player has used up all his cards, the game is over and the other players have to give the winner one match for every card they have left. Any matches not claimed from the horses stay on them until the next game.

Tiddlywinks

For this game you need some plastic tiddlywinks and a cup or bowl. Players take it in turns to flip their small tiddlywinks into the cup. You do this by holding the larger tiddlywink between your thumb and forefinger and pressing down on the edge of the smaller tiddlywink. The aim is to be the first person to get all your tiddlywinks in the bowl. If a tiddlywink lands on top of another, the bottom one can't be used until the top one is played again, so you can stop your opponent from winning by landing on them. If a tiddlywink is leaning against the bowl or cup, it can't be played until it's knocked down.

Chinese whispers

This game is intended for a large group of children and adults – in fact the more the better. The group sits in a large circle. One person starts and whispers a short sentence into the ear of the person sitting to the right of them, for example, 'I like cauliflower'. The sentence is whispered once.

The player then whispers the sentence into the ear of the player to their right, and the game continues. When the sentence reaches the person sitting to the left of the originator the message is announced out loud. The sentence will sound very different! The person to the right starts the game again.

Games you can play in the garden

Most of the games mentioned here don't need expensive equipment. You can save a fortune on things like tennis rackets and croquet sets by buying second hand or on eBay.

Games for big groups

Try these old favourites for large gatherings which children and adults will enjoy equally. Grown-ups who don't want to join in can act as judges. You'll need plenty of space for these games, however.

Sack race

Everyone knows this game where you scramble into a sack and then hop to the finishing line. If you can't get hold of hessian sacks you could use large bin liners or plastic refuse sacks, but make sure they're strong enough.

Three-legged race

Players organize themselves into teams of two, and one teammate ties their right leg to the other teammate's left leg. The teams then have to hobble as fast as they can to the finishing line. (Try to use a piece of fabric instead of rope as this will rub less).

Tug of war

Designate a starting point and draw two lines equidistant from this point. Ensure the middle of the rope is over the starting point for fairness. Two teams then both hang on to the strong length of rope and try to pull the other team across the line. Make sure each team has roughly the same weight of people for fairness. To make it more fun you could have boys versus girls, or dads versus mums, or aunts versus uncles – any combination you like depending on the mix of relations.

Scrambled eggs

Players organize themselves into teams of of two and face each other about 1 metre (3 feet) apart. One player in each team is given an egg which they have to throw to their teammate. If the egg gets dropped, the team is out. If the egg is caught each teammate then takes a big step back and throws the egg again. Play carries on like this, each team taking a step back before every throw, until one team is left with an unbroken egg.

Garden golf

This is played like real golf except that you don't have to mash up your lawn. It can be played in teams of two or four. You'll need a walking stick or putter and a tennis or golf ball. Lay out your golf course with various objects representing holes, such as a flower pot lying on its side or a box with a square cut out of it. Use your imagination! To make it harder, put bunkers (obstacles) on the course such as bricks, garden tools and so on.

Garden skittles

You'll need three tennis balls and ten skittles to play this or you can improvise with empty juice cartons or mineral water bottles. However they should all be the same size and type. The length of the 'alley' depends on the size of the garden and who's playing.

Set the skittles up in the shape of a triangle with four in the back row, three in the second row, two in the third and one at the front. If you only have six skittles arrange them in rows of three, two and one at the front. Leave a space of about 15 centimetres (6 inches) between each skittle and each row.

The winner is the first person to score a previously agreed number of points, say 100. You have three goes at bowling at the skittles. The number you knock down is added to your score. If you knock down all the skittles with your first ball, they are set up again for your next ball. If you knock down all the skittles again, they are set up once more for your last ball. When all the players have had their turns, the first player starts the second round. The game continues in this way until a player reaches the agreed number.

Games you can play sitting down

Here is a collection of games that can be played sitting down, which will please some of the older family members or friends.

Buzz

Another word game which requires a quick brain and knowledge of your five times table. You all sit in a circle and the first player says '1', the next '2', the third '3' and so on until you reach the number 5, when you have to say, 'buzz' instead of '5'. Players carry on counting but every time there's a 5 in the number or a number that 5 can be divided into, you have to say 'buzz'.

Anagrams

You can play this word game as individual players or in teams. To play it you need letter tiles – Scrabble ones are ideal – or if you're feeling very industrious, you can make your own out of card.

Choose a collection of words for your challenge – go for a mix of words to suit the different ages playing. Give each player or team the letter tiles to make their words, and a clue to get them going. The first player or team to unscramble all their words wins.

Ring on a string

This is a simple game that even the very young (four-year-olds) can manage. You thread a slender ring (a wedding ring is ideal) on to a long length of string and tie the ends together. Everybody sits in a circle holding the string – with the guesser in the middle – and, concealing it in their fists, they pass the ring to one another along the string. The guesser calls 'Stop' and the ring has to remain with the person who has it at that moment. The guesser then points to a fist, saying, 'Take that one away' until only the fist holding the ring remains. (Of course, the chances are that the guesser will get it wrong before that happens!) If the person hiding the ring gets discovered, they change places with the guesser. If the guesser gets it wrong, they have to remain in the centre.

Tiddlywinks golf

This is played individually or in pairs. Each player has a large and a small tiddlywink. Lay out a course on the floor or on a table made up of containers of different heights and sizes, for example, an egg cup, a pudding basin, a cup, a small plate. Place bunkers (obstacles) along the course to make it more difficult – these could be books, ornaments etc. The aim is to flip your tiddlywink into the various containers.

Spinning the plate

Another one for all the family and children over the age of six. Find a dinner plate that will spin well and isn't precious (plastic may be the safest option). Everyone sits in a circle and the spinner spins the plate and calls out someone's name. That person has to lunge to the floor and catch the plate before it stops spinning. If he/she fails, they must take over the spinning.

Squeak piggy, squeak

Children love this one because the grown-ups get so giggly. The guesser is blindfolded and handed a cushion. Everyone else takes a seat in a circle around them. The guesser then finds his/her way to a lap and, placing the cushion on it, sits down and orders the person to 'Squeak piggy, squeak'. The 'lap' then squeaks and the guesser has to say who they think it is. If they're correct, the owner of the lap is blindfolded and takes their place.

Stations

Everyone sits in a circle and chooses a station name – perhaps Waterloo or their local station or something preposterous such as Little Neverwallop on the River. A blindfolded person sits in the middle and calls out a switch, for example, 'Victoria change with Waterloo'. These two stations have to change places, creeping past the blindfolded player without being caught. Every so often the blindfolded player will call out 'All change', and everybody must find a new seat. When someone is caught, they must change places with the blindfolded player.

What's in the bag?

This game is played by two teams. Put 12 pairs of identical objects into two bags, such as two batteries, two teaspoons, two buttons, two small oranges and so on in each bag. Don't put anything in that's sharp. Someone shouts 'Go' and the first players from each team have to rummage in the bag and find two matching objects by feel only. If they are successful, they take the objects and pass the bag to the next player who does the same. The winning team is the one which gets the most paired objects

The hat game

You will need:

- hat or other container
- egg timer or stopwatch

- small pieces of paper
- a pencil for each player.

Give each player ten to 15 small pieces of paper and a pencil, and ask them to secretly write down on each piece of paper the name of a famous person or character (alive or dead, real or imaginary). Fold the names up and put them in a hat.

Divide the players into teams. It's best to have no more than three or four teams with no more than three or four players on each team. Try to mix up ages and abilities.

One player is chosen from each team to start, and one team is chosen to begin. At the signal, that player pulls a name from the hat and tries to describe to the other players on his team who that character is, without using any of the names written down. For example, he could describe Superman as 'a hero who works at a newspaper'. As soon as someone guesses the character another name is pulled from the hat. The other teams keep score and watch the time, shouting 'Time's up' after one minute. Carry on until each player has had a turn, count up all the right guesses and declare a winning team.

Song titles

This game is played with two teams. Toss a coin to see which team starts, and then the team that wins the toss begins by singing a song which has a colour in the title. When they've finished singing it, the other team has to respond by singing a song with a colour in it too. The titles you could come up with might be 'Lady in Red', 'Yellow Submarine', 'Lily the Pink', 'Blue Velvet'. The game carries on like this, until a team runs out of ideas. You can choose any subject to sing about, for example, songs about animals or places.

Two noisy games

Up Jenkins

All you need for this fast and furious card game is a five pence (ten cent) piece, or any other small coin, and a pack of old playing cards.

How to play

Two teams sit at opposite sides of a table. One team (Team A) has a five pence piece, which it has to hide from the other team

(Team B), while obeying orders from the leader of the opposing team. Team A starts with a five pence piece which is passed, under the table from hand to hand, until one player keeps it, hidden in his hand. On the order 'Up Jenkins' from the leader of Team B, Team A place their hands on the table, firmly clenched. The leader of Team B tells them to do any one of the following three things:

- Creepy crawly – move fingers forward in a crawling movement.
- Wobbly – clenched hands must be turned over and back on the table.
- Flat on table – hands must be laid down flat on the table.

Team B then has to guess which player in team A has the coin. If they get this right, it's their turn to hide the five pence piece. If they get it wrong, Team A has another turn. The same player can keep the coin or pass it to another player in the team when their hands are under the table again. The game carries on like this until the other team guesses correctly who has the five pence piece.

Pit (3–7 players)

One of the best card games ever and great for livening up the party if older guests are dozing off. Kids will love it as they get to shout a lot! The aim of the game, based on the American Corn Exchange, is to collect, by trading, eight cards in one particular commodity – Barley, Corn, Coffee, Wheat, Oranges, Oats, Soy or Sugar (the original edition has a few different commodities).

How to play

The dealer deals out nine cards to each player. If three people are playing, use three complete suits (for example, Corn, Wheat and Barley, 27 cards). If four are playing, use four suits and so on. Discard all the other cards. Everyone looks at their cards and decides which ones they want to trade in order to collect a particular commodity (you're allowed to trade up to four cards). The dealer presses the bell and says 'The Exchange is open' and everyone starts trading at once, holding out the cards they want to swap (facedown so the other players can't see them) and shouting repeatedly, 'One, One, One!' or 'Two, Two, Two!' etc., depending on how many cards they want to trade. If another player is shouting the same number, the two players swap cards quickly, look at them and resume trading to try and collect the eight cards of one commodity. You can't trade cards of different commodities, for example one Corn card and one Coffee card and a Bear card for two cards. The first person to do this shouts out 'Corner on Sugar!', or whatever commodity it is.

Variation

You can vary the game by adding the Bull and Bear cards when you deal the cards out so two players get an extra card each. The Bull card is a 'wild' card, meaning it can be played as any card you want. This means that if you hold the Bull card you shout 'Bull Corner!' if you have seven cards of one commodity and one card of another. Simply lay down the seven matching cards and Bull card and discard the extra. The Bear card carries a penalty so when you're trading you need to get rid of it as soon as you can. You can do this in the normal way by shouting, for example, 'Three, Three, Three!' and then handing over, say, two Wheat cards and a Bear card.

Murder mystery games

Alibis

This is a game to suit a slightly older family. Players pair up and go into a secret huddle for a strict five minutes to concoct various alibis: what the two players were doing when an imaginary crime was committed, say, between the hours of two and four p.m. on a certain Saturday afternoon. (Avoid a pairing who might actually have been together for a similar two hours and could simply use that scenario – the whole point is to concoct a false alibi.) Everybody then gathers back in the living room for the interrogation. Chosen detectives summon one of each pair and have ten minutes to ask questions such as 'Did you travel by bus or train?' 'Did you meet anyone?' 'What time did you leave?' 'Did you have just coffee or a meal?' (These are the sorts of questions the pair should have anticipated and pre-arranged answers for.) Then the detectives call in the partner and see if he/she comes up with identical answers. If their alibis don't tally, the detectives can claim they're lying… and therefore probably one of them did commit a crime and his partner is trying to cover up for him. The pair with the fewest errors wins the game.

Murder in the dark

The classic Agatha Christie favourite – and amazingly scary, considering you'll be playing with your own family and close friends! (Too scary for young children incidentally.) From a pack of playing cards, extract a King, a Jack and enough other non-picture cards for each of the other people present. Everyone draws a card. The person with the King declares it and he/she is the detective. The others replace their cards without revealing them – including the one who has drawn the Jack and is the murderer.

The detective remains in the one lit room in the house and everyone else disperses and, perhaps, hides. Amid all the squeals and giggles the murderer creeps around and finds a victim and fakes strangulation. The victim lets out a piercing scream and drops dead. From that moment nobody must move – except the murderer, who must make his/her getaway away from the body. The detective times one minute from the scream and then switches on all the lights.

Now the detective interviews everybody one by one. Where were they? Who did they see? Did they witness anyone passing them after the scream and, if so, can they identify them? Everybody must tell the truth – except the murderer, who can fabricate anything he/she likes – even down to saying they actually witnessed the murder committed by Mum! After the interrogations are complete, the detective names the murderer and learns if his/her suspect was indeed guilty.

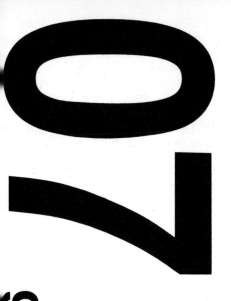

07

getting active

In this chapter you will learn:
- activities you can do in the park, including cycling, football and rounders
- some basic tips on how to ice skate, roller skate and rollerblade
- traditional children's games.

You don't need to be told how important exercise is for children. It not only keeps them fit and healthy, but helps them sleep better and improves their concentration so they're better able to cope with daily life. You know how cranky your own children can get if they've been cooped up all day and not had a chance to let off steam. Children also derive a huge amount of pleasure and satisfaction in physical activities, especially if it's something they really enjoy. But even if your child isn't 'sporty', there are plenty of activities they can engage in which will boost their self-esteem and makes them feel good about themselves. Above all, make exercise fun. Don't turn it into a chore but choose activities that are enjoyable and which all the family can take part in.

Activities for the park

If you're stuck for something to do and the kids are fizzing with energy, there's no better place to take them than your local park. In the safety of a car-free zone they can chase around, play ball games, go rollerblading, play hide and seek – all the time using up their bountiful energy. Playgrounds with swings, slides and climbing frames are excellent for younger children.

Cycling

Cycling is one of the easiest and most enjoyable activities to engage in as a family. Apart from the obvious health benefits, it does wonders for children's sense of independence, giving their confidence a terrific boost. It's also a great social activity. Make family cycle rides part of your regular routine. Don't just stick to the well-known routes but go on expeditions further afield. Cycling in the countryside is infinitely preferable and far less stressful than cycling in the town. Wherever you cycle, make sure you all wear cycling helmets and everyone's bike is in full working order, with tyres pumped up and brakes and lights working. If you're doing any cycling on roads, make sure your children know the basic rules of cycling on the road. It's a very good idea to enrol them on a cycling proficiency course.

Football

The beauty about football is that it's such a versatile sport. You can play it with a full team of 11 players, play five-a-side, set up an impromptu game with two or more players, or simply practise your football skills on your own. All you need to play it is two goal posts (jumpers on the ground will do) and a football. More and more girls are playing football although it remains most popular with boys. If your child is keen on the game, keep that interest alive by enrolling them in a local team.

French cricket (2 or more players)

All you need to play this very simple game is a cricket bat and a tennis ball. One person bats and everyone else fields. As the batsman you're not allowed to move but have to stand still with your feet together. The fielders bowl balls overarm (or underarm for little children) at the batsman, and try to hit the batsman's legs ('stumps') below the knees. They can bowl the ball from wherever they field it, which can make it quite hard for the batsman to hit the ball back when they can't move their feet. However, if they hit the ball they are allowed to turn and face a different direction. As the batsman, you can use your bat anywhere around your legs to stop the ball from hitting you and you can hit the ball in any direction. You are out if the ball hits your legs or if another player catches the ball before it bounces. The next batsman is the player who caught or stumped you out. You score runs by passing the bat around your body, swapping hands when it's behind your back. Each 'round' counts as one run.

Rounders (8 or more players)

Rounders is very similar to baseball and is an ideal game for large groups. The batsman has to hit the ball and run around all the bases in order to score a rounder, without being caught or stumped out.

You will need:

- six cones for bases
- a rounders bat (or short baseball bat)
- a small ball.

How to play

Players divide into two teams; one batting, the other fielding. Toss a coin to see which side bats. If you're batting first, take up the batsman's position (see figure 22) while the other players wait for their turn. The opposing team chooses who is going to bowl first, and four players stand at the four bases – one player at first base, another at second base, a third at third base and a fourth player at fourth base. The backstop (BS) stands behind the batsman in line with the bowler and is there to catch any balls the batsman misses. The rest of the fielding team stand behind the bases, ready to catch or field the ball. There aren't any boundaries so they can stand where they want (figure 22).

The bowler bowls the ball at you, and you have three attempts to hit the ball. You have to run if you hit the ball; if you miss it you don't have to run, but have to run after the third ball whether you miss it or not. If you choose to run when you miss the ball you can only go to first base; this also applies if you miss the third ball. If you hit the ball and it goes behind you, the backstop or referee shouts 'First base only' and that's as far as you're allowed to go.

Here's illustration of how the game works: say you hit a blinder which goes soaring out into the field. You attempt to get a rounder by running like mad to each base in turn, touching each one with your bat and shouting 'first base', 'second base', 'third base' and 'fourth base' as you go. Meanwhile, the fielders scurry around trying to retrieve the ball. Whoever picks it up throws it to a player manning the base you're trying to run to, with the aim of stumping you out. For example, if you're haring towards

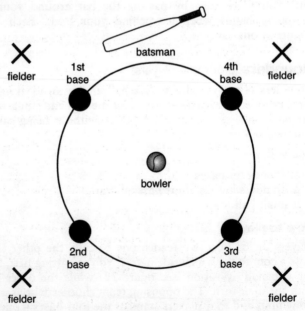

figure 22 the positions on a rounder's pitch

second base but the player there catches the ball and 'stumps' or touches the base before you reach it, you are out.

You must only run to the next base if you think you can get there before the ball does. If not, you must remain at the base you got to, and finish running round when somebody else bats. You can only run once the next ball is thrown. Everyone has to stop running if the bowler holds the ball and shouts 'All stop!' If you're running round you can't overtake any player in front of you or be on the same base as another player in your team. If you stop at a base because the one in front in your team has been stumped you can be run out if the player behind you runs to your base. Once you've left a base you can't go back to it. If a player is run out or caught out they have to stop batting for that round. When all the batters are out, it's the fielding team's turn to bat. Each time a player makes it all the way round without getting stumped out, a 'rounder' is scored for the team. These are added up at the end to determine the winner.

Get your skates on

Ice skating

There's nothing to beat ice skating outdoors on a frosty winter's day and these days there is a wealth of public skating rinks where the whole family can skate safely.

If you haven't skated before, it's not that hard to learn. You just need confidence and not to worry about falling over. Make sure you wear the right clothes and always warm up before a session. You also need to learn how to fall without hurting yourself. If you feel yourself losing your balance, do your best to fall on your bottom or side and tuck your hands in to avoid injury from other skaters. To get up, kneel with your hands flat on the ice. Place one foot on the ice and then the other, so your weight is evenly distributed between both feet, and gradually straighten up.

Once you can fall safely, you can learn some basic skating techniques. Start marching with small steps, then as you get a little faster, allow yourself to glide forward on both feet. Shift your weight to your right foot and glide briefly. Practise gliding on one foot, coming back to a two-foot glide, and then gliding with the other foot.

To stop, glide forward on one skate and position the other skate behind it and at a right angle to it, so stopping with your feet in a 'T' shape.

Top ice skating rinks around the world

UK, London Somerset House. This ice rink in the romantic eighteenth-century courtyard of Somerset House has become one of London's most popular ice rinks. Other good ice rinks include Canary Wharf, The National History Museum, the Tower of London, Hyde Park, Kew Gardens, Greenwich and Hampton Court Palace. For more information visit **www.enjoyengland.com**.

USA, New York The Rockefeller Centre rink is the USA's most famous Christmas ice rink. For more information about ice rinks throughout the USA, visit **www.usatourist.com**.

USA, Los Angeles This vast outdoor ice rink in Pershing Square is surrounded by soaring skyscrapers in downtown LA.

USA, Yosemite National Park The Curry Village ice rink is set against the backdrop of Yosemite's most dramatic sights – Half Dome and Glacier Point.

Finland, Helsinki As you would expect in such a snow-bound country, ice skating is a national hobby and Finland has a huge number of outdoor rinks. A rink also opens over Christmas in Helsinki.

France, Paris The Stade de France national stadium is transformed into the Rêve de Neige (snow dream), a winter sports resort with two huge ice rinks, and loads of other activities including snowboarding ramps, skiing pistes, ice-climbing walls, snowman building areas and sledging runs.

Russia, Moscow The city has seven indoor and 11 outdoor rinks. At Gorky Park's huge skating rink you can try your hand (or feet) at a Russian ice disco.

Germany, Berlin In Potsdamer Platz you'll find a 40 metre-long ice rink, a snow park and Christmas market. Kids will love the sledging slope which you can slide or ski down.

Roller skating

Find a wide, open place to practise with a smooth surface such as an empty car park. Before you start, make sure you're wearing proper safety gear, including helmet, knee, wrist and elbow guards and hand gloves. After you've warmed up, stand up with your knees slightly bent and your heels together and toes out. Stretch your arms out to help you balance. Put your right foot forward and then your left foot. Go slowly at first, just slightly lifting your foot.

If you feel yourself falling, keep your hands out in front of you, bend your knees as much as possible and fall on your bottom or side. Try not to break your fall with your hands or you could injure them.

Learn how to use the T-stop technique to stop (see figure 23). As your right foot continues forward, bring your left foot back to make a right angle with your right foot (as with ice skating).

figure 23 using the T-stop technique to stop

Rollerblading

Rollerblading, or 'in-line skating', is similar to ice skating. You use a technique called the 'stride' to get started, which is a sort of pushing and gliding movement. This does take a lot of practice, but once you've mastered the movement, you're well on the way to picking up speed and other moves to enable you to travel along quite happily!

It's crucial that you wear the proper protective equipment at all times. This means kneepads, elbow pads, wrist pads and a crash helmet.

How to move

Put your feet together and turn your toes out so you're standing with your feet in a 'V' position. Bend your knees a little and your body should lean in the direction in which you want to move. Practise pushing your right foot out to the side, then return it to the 'V' position, then do the same with the left skate.

How to push off

As you push off with your left skate, put your weight on your right foot and you'll find that this movement pushes you forward. Then, as you lift your left foot, allow your right skate to just glide along the ground. Bring your feet together and put your weight on the balls of your feet to enable you to recover your balance. At this point, your feet should not be in the V position, but instead your skates should be roughly shoulder width apart.

Now, try pushing off with your right foot and letting the left skate glide along the ground. Then return to the position described above, where you regain your balance by balancing your weight on the balls of your feet. When you have done this a few times, omit the balance position between and try to link the pushing and gliding movements from both your feet together.

How to stop

It's vital to learn how to stop when you're rollerblading. One of your skates will have a rubber stop on the heel. As you're gliding, bring this skate forward so that the brake is level with the front wheel of your back skate. Lift the toe of the braking skate until you feel the brake gently touch the ground, and keep increasing this pressure as you glide along. Don't put all your weight onto it at once, and make sure you keep looking straight ahead – if you look down at your skates you'll be more inclined to lose your balance. When the braking skate is in position on the ground, bend the knee of the back leg. This will give you greater control over the brake, as if you are sitting back on it.

How to fall

When you start learning how to rollerblade, you're bound to lose your balance more than a few times. However, if you fall in the right way, this need not be a great problem. Always try to fall forward rather than back, and bend at the waist to reduce the impact of the fall.

Even though it sounds silly, do try to stay relaxed. Try also to direct the impact of the fall onto your kneepads, so aim to land first on your knees then your elbows and wrists. Try not to let your head hit the ground – keep it up, and stretch your arms out as you fall, so that you slide along the ground – your protective equipment will help spread the impact over your body.

Traditional games

Skipping

It's great exercise, costs next to nothing and you can do it virtually anywhere. Skipping is one of those overlooked games of yesteryear when children used the street as their playground. They would stretch the rope across the street, tying one end to a lamp post and skip for hours, making up chants and rhymes to go with their skipping-rope games.

You can skip on your own or with other people. Skipping with other people involves two people turning the rope and one person skipping. The turners need to turn the rope so it goes high enough over the jumper and low enough to hit the ground so the jumper can step or jump over it. The turners have a lot of control – they can turn the rope faster or slower, and try and get the skipper out.

Skipping rhymes

There are a number of songs to sing whilst skipping, here are some examples.

Two Little Dickie Birds

Two people turn the rope and two players skip in it.

Two little dickie birds sitting on the wall (*two players jump in*)
One named Peter, one named Paul (*both players wave at their name*)

Fly away, Peter, fly away, Paul (*the player exits the rope as their name is called*)
Don't you come back 'till your birthday's called
January, February... December (*the player returns when their month is called*)
Now fly away, fly away, fly away (*both players exit the rope*).

Jelly on the Plate

Jelly on the plate
Jelly on the plate
Wibble wobble (*the jumper wobbles while skipping and tries not to overbalance*)
Wibble, wobble
Jelly on the plate.

Salt and mustard

For this game you have two turners, and several jumpers who jump at the same time. The skippers jump over the revolving rope, chanting repeatedly 'Salt, mustard, vinegar, pepper.' Each time they say 'pepper' the rope gets faster. As people fail to jump the rope they have to stop jumping and sit out. The last one in is the winner.

ABC

Two turners turn the rope as the other person jumps. As he/she jumps they sing:

Strawberry, shortcake, treacle tart
Tell me the name of your sweetheart
A B C D E...

The letter you fail to jump the rope on, is the initial of your sweetheart.

Teddy Bear, Teddy Bear

Two turners turn the rope and another person jumps the rope and chants the rhyme, doing the actions to each line.

Teddy Bear, Teddy Bear touch the ground (*touch the ground while skipping*)
Teddy Bear, Teddy Bear turn around (*turn around*)
Teddy Bear, Teddy Bear climb the stairs (*pretend to walk up stairs while skipping*)
Teddy Bear, Teddy Bear say your prayers (*join hands to say prayers while skipping*)
Teddy Bear, Teddy Bear turn off the lights (*reach up to turn off a light*)
Teddy Bear, Teddy Bear say good night (*wave and say 'Good Night' as you skip out of the rope*)

The next skipper comes in and the rhyme starts again.

Skipping moves

Can Can

Jump on your left foot and raise your right knee at the same time. Then jump with both feet. Jump on your left foot again and kick your right foot at the same time. Then jump with both feet. Repeat with the other leg.

Pretzel

Skip on one leg, bending the other leg and holding it with your hand.

Double Dutch

Two ropes are turned in opposite directions and the skipper has to enter the ropes and skip both ropes. More than one person can be inside the ropes at once.

Hopscotch

This was a hugely popular street game in Victorian England and was known by lots of different names. In Scotland it was known as Peever or Beds and was played in a variety of ways. Today it's still played all over the world. The pattern may vary, but the game is pretty similar wherever you go.

How to play

Draw a hopscotch pattern in chalk on the ground, or make your own indoors by creating a grid with wide masking tape. (Don't let your children draw on public pavements, however, as this could be classed as graffiti.) The pattern consists of eight boxes, numbered 1 to 8 (although in some places there are ten boxes, numbered 1 to 10). For instance, your grid could consist of 1, 2 and 3 in a line, 4 and 5 next to each other, 6 on its own and 7 and 8 next to each other at the top (see figure 24).

Each player has a marker – this could be a stone, a button or a bottle cap, but they need to look different. Stand behind the square 1 and throw your marker into it. Hop over square 1 to square 2 and then continue hopping to square 8, turn around, and hop back again. Pause in square 2 to pick up your marker, hop in square 1, and out. Then continue by tossing the stone in square 2. You must always hop on one foot, unless the hopscotch pattern has two squares next to each other. In this case, you can put two feet down, one in each square. A player must always hop over any square where a marker has been placed. You're out if your marker misses the right square; you step on a line or lose your balance when picking up the marker;

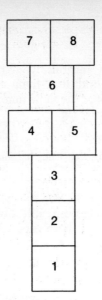

figure 24 an example of a hopscotch grid

and put a second hand or foot down; you hop into a square with a marker, or put two feet down in a single box. At the end of your go you put the marker in the square where you will resume playing on your next turn, and then the next player begins.

In some versions of hopscotch, a semi-circle is added at the far end of the pattern (beyond the 7 and 8) where the player can rest before hopping back through.

Marbles

These are the rules for a version of 'ring taw' marbles, an older, more common variant. There are many other ways to play.

How to play

Draw a circle about 1 metre (3 feet) in diameter – use chalk on asphalt or concrete, a stick in dirt, or a string on carpet or tiles. Select your shooter – your biggest marble which you'll use to hit targets out of the ring – and place your target marbles inside the circle; the other players do the same. Everyone places the same amount of marbles in the ring. As well as being the largest, your shooter needs to look distinctive, so you can easily identify it.

The order of play can be decided by 'lagging'. Players line up opposite a line 3 metres (10 feet) away (the 'lag line') and shoot their marbles at it. The player whose marble ends up closest to the line goes first, the next closest goes second, and so on.

When it's your go, kneel down and hold your shooter in one hand. Flicking it out of your fist with your thumb, shoot it from outside the ring at one or more marbles in the ring. If you knock any marbles out of the ring and your shooter is still inside it, you take another shot from wherever your shooter is placed. If you fail to do this and/or your shooter remains in the ring, it's the next player's turn. Players take turns to shoot until the ring is empty. The winner is the player with the most marbles at the end of the game. The owners reclaim their marbles unless you're playing 'keepsies', where players keep the marbles they won during the game.

Jacks

All you need to play this is five jacks and one ball. Jacks are the modern equivalent of knucklebones or stones from which this game derives.

How to play

You need two players for this game. To decide who starts, a player throws five jacks into the air with one hand and tries to catch as many as possible on the back of the same hand. The jacks that were caught are then thrown up again from the back of the hand where they came to rest and as many as possible are caught in the palm of the same hand. The other players do the same and the player who catches the most jacks starts, play continuing in a clockwise fashion.

The first player prepares to start by throwing the five jacks on the ground. He/she then throws the ball up, picks up one jack with the same hand and then catches the ball before it hits the ground. The jack is then put into the other hand. This is repeated until all the jacks have been picked up. The player then throws the jacks back on the floor and starts again, but this time, two jacks must be picked up each time except for the third and final throw when, obviously, only one jack is picked up. Once this is achieved successfully, the player starts again but this time with three jacks and then again with four jacks and finally the ball is thrown up and all five jacks must be picked up at once before the ball is caught. Remember, only the one hand can be used.

When a player misses the ball or doesn't manage to pick up the right number of jacks, it's the next player's turn. The player who manages to get furthest in the sequence of throws wins.

Chasing games

These games involve tearing around and avoiding being caught, and are great for children of all ages. Can be played with two or more players.

Duck, duck, goose

You sit down in a circle facing each other. One person is 'It' and walks around the circle. As they walk around, they tap people's heads and say whether they are a 'duck' or a 'goose'. Once someone is the 'goose' they get up and try to chase the person who is 'It' around the circle. The aim is to tap that person before they are able sit down in the 'goose's' spot. If the goose is not able to do this, they become 'It' for the next round and play continues. If they do tap the 'It' person, the person tagged has to sit in the centre of the circle. Then the goose becomes 'It' for the next round. The person in the middle can't leave until another person is tagged and they are replaced.

It/Tag

The simplest game ever and one of the best. One player is 'It' and chases after the rest of the players, trying to catch one of them by touching them. If you touch a player you say 'You're It' and then they start chasing after everyone. There are all sorts of different variations of this game as you can imagine:

Chain tag

One player is 'It' and runs after the other players, trying to catch someone. As soon as he/she succeeds, the caught player links arms with the player who is 'It' and they charge round trying to catch a third player. If they succeed, this player links arms with the other two and they try to catch the next player. The game continues until just one player is left.

Shadow tag

You catch someone by stepping on their shadow so you need to play this in the sunshine.

Touch tag

One player is 'It' and chooses something made of a particular substance that the other players can touch to protect them against being caught. For instance, if you're 'It' and choose wood, you shout out 'wood!' and the other players have to touch something made of wood, such as a tree, to stop them being caught. However, only one player is allowed to be in each particular spot to protect them from being caught. Anyone not touching anything made of wood can be caught. They are then 'It' and have to shout out another word, such as 'glass' which the players can touch to keep safe.

Off ground tag

In this game of tag, the people being chased cannot be tagged by the chaser if they are off the ground – such as standing on a bench or a brick, or hanging from a branch. Obviously you can only play this game somewhere where there are enough things to stand on. Care must be taken when climbing on objects.

Tunnel tag

If a player is tagged (touched), they have to stand still with their legs apart. They can be freed by another player crawling through their legs, but of course there's always the risk that that player might get tagged in the process.

TV tag

In this variation, when the person who is 'It' tags someone, that person has to stand stock still. To be able to move, someone must touch them and yell out the name of a TV show. The name can only be used once. Play continues until everyone is standing motionless. The last person to be tagged is 'It' for the next game. You can also play this using any other category, for example, movie tag, or football team tag.

What's the time, Mr Wolf?

One player chooses to be Mr Wolf and the rest of the players line up a few feet away from him. Mr Wolf has his back to them and the players begin to creep forward towards him. With every step they take, one of the players asks 'What's the time, Mr Wolf?' He answers, 'Two o'clock' or whatever time he likes, and the players continue to creep forward, with every step asking the time and getting a response. Until… at any point in the game their question, 'What's the time, Mr Wolf?' is answered by a roar, 'Dinnertime!' and Mr Wolf turns around and chases the players. Whoever he catches is the next Mr Wolf.

Mother, may I?

This is similar to Mr Wolf, but instead of Mr Wolf, the player chosen to be Mother stands with his or her back to the rest of the players. They stand a reasonable distance away (but not too far so Mother can't hear them). Mother gives orders to each player in turn, for example, 'Mary, take one giant step' or 'Tom, take three bunny steps'. Before carrying out the order, the player must always say, 'Mother, May I?' Mother can then say 'Yes' or 'No'. If the player forgets to make this request, he or she has to go back to the start. Play continues like this, with Mother giving orders to other players, until one player reaches the place where Mother is standing and becomes Mother.

A word about the different steps and what they mean:

Baby step – tiny step forward
Giant step – large step forward
Ballet step – spinning in a circle
Banana step – the player lays down and marks where his/her head is and then stands there
Bunny step – hop forward
Scissors step – jump forward while crossing feet. If you have to do more than one scissor step, you can uncross your feet when you jump forward.

Red light, green light

One player is chosen to be the red or stop light and stands facing away from the rest of the players, who line up 3–4 metres (10–15 feet) away. When the stop light says 'Green light' the players are allowed to move forward. When the stop light says 'Red light' and turns around, any player caught moving is out. The game continues when the stop light says 'Green light'. The first player to touch the stop light wins the game and becomes the stop light for the next game. However, if no one manages to touch the stop light, the stop light is the winner.

Ball games

Piggy in the middle

For this you will need three players: two players stand opposite each other with another player in the middle. The two players begin throwing the ball to each other, while the middle player has to try to intercept the ball. If they succeed, the player who threw the ball is the next Piggy in the middle.

Broken bottles (4 or more players)

Players stand in a circle and throw a ball to each other. If you miss or drop the ball you have to pay a forfeit. Forfeits run in the following order:

- First: throw with only one hand
- Second: with the opposite hand
- Third: kneeling on one knee
- Fourth: on both knees
- Fifth: lying flat.

After the fifth forfeit you're out. If you catch the ball you can get up again, in reverse order. The winner is the player who manages to stay in longest.

Simple dodge ball

Divide children into two teams. Try to throw a small soft ball below the waist of someone in the opposite team (you can throw in the ordinary way to someone on your own team). If you hit that person, he's out. The team with the last remaining person wins.

Wall games

Ball games played against a wall have always been popular and it's easy to see why.

Donkey

This can be played with two or more players. The players line up facing a wall – about 2 metres (6 feet) from it. One player is chosen to throw the ball at the wall and, as it bounces back, everyone has to jump over it. If a player is hit or touched by the ball they gain a letter, eventually spelling DONKEY. The player who makes the whole word after being hit six times is out. The winner is the player with the least amount of letters. Time each game so everyone can have a turn at throwing. Keep a score sheet to see who is the overall winner.

Sevens

You can play this on your own or with other players. The rules couldn't be simpler – you throw the ball seven times in seven different ways:

1 Throw the ball against the wall and catch it.
2 Throw the ball against the wall, turning around once before catching it.
3 Pat the ball against the wall seven times without catching it full
4 Bounce the ball seven times at the wall and catch it.
5 Bounce the ball under one leg and against the wall and catch it.
6 Throw the ball against the wall, let it bounce then catch it.
7 Throw the ball against the wall with one arm behind your back and catch it.

Games for large groups

Bom bom bom

You need two teams, each with a captain. Each team has a home base. After teams are chosen, one team is chosen to present the charade. This team then decides what to do, for example, 'wash dishes', 'wash clothes', 'ride a horse' or 'go grocery shopping' etc. Once this has been done and the actions for the charade have been discussed, the teams line up on their home bases facing each other. The teams then approach each other and the team chosen to begin the game, starts with the following:

Team 1: 'Here we come.'
Team 2: 'Where are you from?'
Team 1: 'New Orleans.'
Team 2: 'What's your trade?'
Team 1: 'Ice cream and lemonade.'

Team 1 then begins the charade and Team 2 tries to guess it. The captain of Team 1 answers the guesses either by saying 'Yes' or 'No' or 'You're getting warm', 'You're getting closer', 'You're going to burn', etc. If the correct guess is made, Team 2 tries to catch the members of Team 1 before they can run back to their home base. If everyone in Team 1 reaches their home base without being caught they present another charade. If anyone gets caught, Team 2 presents the charade and the game starts again.

Capture the flag

The object of the game is to capture the other team's flag. All you need to play it is a large area with some good hiding places, plus a couple of flags, which can be anything bright such as a T-shirt.

The players divide into two teams and each team occupies half of the area. (If you have a front and back garden one team could occupy the back, the other team the front.) Each team is given a time limit, say five minutes, to hide their flag in their territory, and also to choose a place for the jail for any prisoners they may catch. During this time both teams send out spies to try to find out where the opponent's flag is hidden, and also appoint lookouts to intercept spies. Once the teams have hidden the flag they call out that they are ready.

Each team now tries to capture the other team's flag by creeping stealthily into each other's territory. Any team member caught trespassing is taken to the jail and remains there until grabbed by another team member. The first team to capture the flag and bring it back to their side wins.

08

high days and holidays

In this chapter you will learn:
- some traditional games including hula hoop, chess and cribbage
- how to juggle and do card tricks
- how to encourage your children to take an interest in nature, for example, by making a birdfeeder or bird table.

School holidays and half-term can be a real headache for parents. You need to find things to occupy your children but it can be hard work getting them out of bed, let alone out of the house. However, there are lots of interesting games and activities you can involve them in that will hold their interest and give you a bit of breathing space. The longer holidays also present an ideal opportunity to introduce your children to pursuits that could well develop into a long-lasting interest, whether it's learning an instrument or a sport. The key is to find something that will suit their nature.

Focus on one or two projects you can make with your child over the holidays or half-term. This could be as simple or ambitious as you like (depending on your own DIY skills). Together you could make a bird table, a nesting box, a tree house, even a rabbit hutch. It doesn't really matter what you make, but by working with you and learning new skills on the way, your child will learn valuable lessons about teamwork and also gain some practical skills. And perhaps, most importantly, you will be teaching your children to take pride in their achievements, and that by putting effort into a project you end up with something which you can justifiably feel proud of.

If time is short, even playing a game of Monopoly or draughts with your children is an enjoyable way of spending time with them. It can also be a big help linking up with other parents and sharing the child care, especially if you have to work or just have one child.

Traditional games

Hula hoop

Your children may never have heard of a hula hoop, but at the height of its popularity in the 1950s and 1960s, 'hooping' was a worldwide craze. Hula hoops can actually be traced back to ancient Egypt when children made them out of dried grape vines.

How to do it

Hooping is a brilliant aerobic exercise for all the family (and a wonderful waist whittler) although it takes a little bit of practice. Stand up straight, with your feet slightly apart. Hold the hula hoop with both hands and place it around your waist, pulling it forward so it rests against your back. Spin the hula hoop in an anti-clockwise motion with your hands and let go. To keep the hoop going, shift your weight back and forth on your feet. Maintain this rocking motion and the hula hoop should spin around just above your hips. It may take a while to keep the hula hoop rotating for long periods of time, but keep practising.

Once you've mastered the basics of hula hooping, you can move on to more advanced techniques. Try keeping the hula hoop spinning around your knees. To begin, stand straight with your legs and feet together and hold the hoop at knee level, so it's resting against the back of your knees. Give the hula hoop a twirl and spread your arms out for balance. Move your knees forward and back as the hoop rotates, and it should spin just above your knees.

And the final challenge for a hula hooper – to keep more than one hoop going. Follow the instructions above, but add another hoop. On your first go, try two hula hoops and then work up to three after you can keep two going, and so on. Don't be discouraged if you find this hard – it does require a lot of practise.

Patience/Solitaire

If you learn one card game this should be it. It should be compulsory for everyone to learn patience or solitaire. It's a game for one, is endlessly entertaining, can be played anywhere and there are over 150 games to learn, ranging from the very easy to the fiendishly hard.

Klondike

This is the most popular version of Solitaire. The aim is to build up all the cards in sequence from Ace to King (Ace, 2, 3, 4, 5, 6, 7, 8, 9, 10, Jack, Queen, King).

Deal out 28 cards in seven columns face down as follows: the first column has one card, the second column has two cards, the third column has three cards and so on up, ending with seven cards in the last column. Place the cards so they overlap and turn over the card at the bottom of each column so it's face up. (See figure 25.)

These seven columns are called the tableau. Place the remaining cards to the left of the tableau to form your stockpile. Leave four spaces above the tableau for the foundation: this is where you will build up your four suits (Hearts, Diamonds, Clubs and Spades) in ascending order, beginning with Aces.

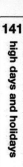

figure 25 the basic layout of Klondike

How to play

To build up the foundation, you need to uncover the facedown cards in the tableau, so you can play them. You do this by moving tableau cards onto the foundation and onto other columns in the tableau. Look at the face up cards in the tableau and see if you can move any cards onto other columns. Cards on the tableau are built down (i.e. in descending order) in alternating colours (red and black or black and red). So, for instance, you can place a red 8 onto a black 9, or a black 10 onto a red Jack. Remember that the King is high and the Ace is low so you can't place a King on an Ace.

When you move a face up card, you can then turn the next card in the column face up. You can move cards in sequence in a column altogether. So, for example, if in one of your columns you had a sequence of 10 of Spades, 9 of Diamonds, 8 of Clubs, 7 of Diamonds and 6 of Spades, you can move them all onto a red Jack. Bear in mind all the time that you're aiming to build up the foundation, so as soon as you uncover an Ace, place it in one of the four gaps above the tableau. If, for example, it's the Ace of Hearts, you're now looking for a 2 of Hearts to carry on building up the foundation, along with the other three Aces.

If you get stuck and can't make any more moves on the tableau and foundation, turn over the top card of the stockpile and place it face-up to form the discard pile. If you can place that card onto the foundation, you can do so. (Try and build up the four foundation piles as evenly as possible. If one foundation pile has more than a couple more cards in it than the other foundation piles, you may not have foundation cards to use in the tableau for building sequences, moving cards and uncovering the face-down cards.)

With this game, you can take cards off the foundation and place them on the tableau. The top card from the discard pile may also be placed onto a tableau column, as long as it follows a valid sequence. You can fill gaps in the tableau (empty columns) with any available King or a sequence starting with the King.

Continue playing in this way. Move cards from the discard pile to the tableau and the foundation; from the tableau to the foundation and within the tableau; and occasionally from the foundation back to the tableau, trying to uncover face-down tableau cards and move them to the foundation. When the stockpile is empty, pick up the discard pile and turn it over (face down) to form a new stockpile.

Two skills to impress family and friends

Here are two easy skills for the children to master in the holidays or when they have time on their hands.

Juggling with three balls

Juggling is one of those accomplishments which never fails to impress people. Teach your children how to juggle and you'll not only be adding to their repertoire of skills, but helping to boost their hand-eye coordination and mental agility. It's also something you can do anywhere, it doesn't require expensive equipment and can be done using almost anything. Although you might think that learning to juggle with three balls is difficult, it doesn't take that long to learn. It's just a question of practise, and more practise!

How to do it

Follow the step-by-step guide opposite and you'll be juggling with three balls before you know it. Go through the steps steadily and carefully. Once you've mastered Step 1 you can do it with your eyes closed (or in your sleep!), move on to Step 2 and then 3. The important thing is not to rush it. There's no need to buy juggling balls at this stage – you can use tennis balls or similar – although using the real thing can make you feel more professional. Juggling balls come in all sorts of weights, colours and sizes, but as a beginner, choose ones filled with seeds, as they're light, easy to handle for smaller hands, and not expensive. Once you've got the hang of juggling, you can move on to more exciting varieties such as ones which glow in the dark.

Learning the Cascade

The Cascade is the best known of the three-ball patterns. It looks very impressive but isn't hard to master.

Step 1 Begin with one ball. Throw it from hand to hand in an arching shape, the highest point at eye level. Practise this over and over, and make sure that your throws from both hands are of the same height and strength. Bear in mind that your dominant hand (i.e. the hand you favour, usually the right) will be stronger than your other hand, so you need extra practise throwing with your weaker hand. When this throw becomes second nature, you can move on to Step 2.

Step 2 Pick up a second ball. Hold one ball in each hand, and just like Step 1, throw ball 1 up in an arch shape. As ball 1 reaches the top of the arch (at eye level), throw ball 2 underneath it. The two balls should cross in the air and change hands. Repeat this stage over and over again, starting to throw with one hand and then with the other. (see figures 26(a) and (b).) When you can do this easily, you can move on to Step 3.

Step 3 Keep hold of balls 1 and 2, and put ball 3 in your dominant hand. Now you have two balls in your strong hand and one in your weaker hand. Begin as you did with two balls, throwing ball 1 (from your strong hand) up in an arch. As it reaches the top of the arch throw ball 2 underneath, as you did before. As ball 2 reaches the top, throw ball 3 underneath it. (See figure 26(c)) Practise over and over, and establish a regular rhythm: 1...2...3...1...2...3... Counting out loud can help. And like magic, you're juggling!

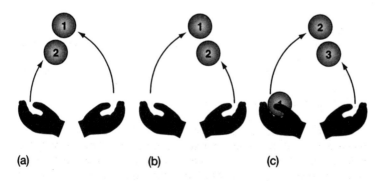

(a)   (b)   (c)

figure 26 juggling with three balls

Easy card tricks

What a result!

You can't go wrong with this easy card trick. No matter how many times you repeat it, the surprising result is always the same. From a pack of playing cards, openly remove five red and five black cards, (it's best to keep to spot cards though not essential) and discard the rest of the pack.

Put the two stacks of cards face to face, with all the cards of one colour together face up and all the cards of the other colour face down on top of them. Thoroughly mix the cards, using an overhand shuffle (see p. 42), taking care that none of the cards turn over while you do this.

Place them behind your back and count off the top five cards, turning this stack of five over. Bring both stacks round to the front again. Spread them in two separate lines along the table and there will be an equal number of face-up cards in each pile. But they will all be alike in colour in each pile.

Reverse one of the stacks and place the two piles together again, shuffle and put them behind your back as before and repeat. Exactly the same thing will happen again.

Magic prediction

To do this trick, you need at least four people – the bigger the audience, the more impressive the trick – plus four or more small pieces of paper (according to how many people are involved), a pen, an A4 piece of card and a hat.

Ask everyone to shout out names of celebrities, living or dead, and as they're called out write each name on a piece of paper which you fold up and place in a hat. Mix up all the pieces of paper, and on the card write down your 'prediction' of the name you're going to pull out of the hat. Ask someone to remove one of the pieces of paper and read out the name written on it. Amazingly, it will be the name that you predicted!

How it's done

The secret to this clever trick is very simple – you write down the first name that's called out and keep writing this name on all the subsequent pieces of paper, regardless of what's called out. For instance, if the first name called out is Madonna, you write Madonna on every piece of paper, even though people are yelling different names. This way you end up with all the pieces of paper in the hat bearing the same name, Madonna. Make a big show of writing your own prediction – which will of course be Madonna – on the card. Put the card somewhere where the audience can see it but not read the name.

Now announce that you will predict the name about to be pulled out of the hat. Ask someone to mix up the papers in the hat, take one out and then read it aloud. With a flourish, show the audience your card with the same name written on it. Admiring gasps will reverbate all round. But make sure you get rid of all the other pieces of paper in the hat or you will be rumbled. (You could ask an accomplice to do this while the audience are momentarily distracted trying to work out how you did this trick.)

All in the mind

A classic trick to try on a friend where you appear to read the mind of your volunteer.

1 Ask your friend to choose a number between 2 and 9.

2 Tell them to take the number that they've chosen and multiply it by 9.

3 This should give them a two-digit number. Ask them to add the two digits of the number together. For example, if their number is 10 take the one and nought and add them to make 1.

4 Tell them to subtract five from the resulting number.

5 Ask them to take the number they now have and make it match a letter in the alphabet, i.e. A=1, B=2, C=3, D=4 and so on.

6 Ask your friend to take their letter and think of a country that begins with that letter. For example, 'B' might make them think of Belgium, 'D' could be Denmark or 'F could be France.

7 Tell them to take the second letter in the name of that country and associate it with an animal. For example, 'P' may go with penguin and 'Z' may associate with zebra.

8 Ask your friend if they now have a country and an animal and tell them that they have to hold those thoughts in their mind while you concentrate on reading their mind.

9 Ask your friend in a puzzled voice, 'Are there really elephants in Denmark?'

How is it done?

For some strange reason, with this mathematical formula you will always end up with the number 4, so people will have to come up with the letter 'D'. They are most likely to think of Denmark for a country, and elephant for the letter 'E'.

More challenging games for older children

Backgammon

You might not think so but the ancient game of backgammon is surprisingly easy to play. While the rules might sound complicated, they're not that hard to learn. As long as you bear in mind that this is a game of strategy as much as luck, you should find it a fascinating and addictive game.

The game is played with two players on a special board with 24 narrow triangles called 'points' in alternate colours, numbered 1–24. The board is divided into four sections, each one containing six points. The bottom right-hand section is your 'home board'; the top right-hand section is your opponent's home board. The two sections on the left are known as the 'outer board'. Each player begins with 15 checkers in two different colours.

The aim of the game is to move your checkers into your home board and then move or 'bear' the checkers off the board. Your moves are determined by rolling the dice. You move one way, from one end of the board to the other through the points. Your white pieces move clockwise, while your black pieces move anti-clockwise.

How to play

To begin, each player throws a single die to decide who starts. (After the first roll, the players throw two dice.) The player with the highest number moves his checkers according to the numbers showing on both dice. The checkers are always moved forward, to a lower-numbered point. You can only move a checker to an 'open' point, one not occupied by two or more 'enemy' checkers.

Rolling the dice

The numbers on the two dice represent separate moves. For example, if you roll 4 and 2, you can move one checker four spaces to an open point and another checker two spaces to an open point, or you can move one checker a total of six spaces to an open point, but only if the intermediate point (either two or four spaces from the starting point) is also open.

If you roll doubles you play the numbers on the dice twice, so a roll of 6 and 6 gives you four sixes to use.

You have to play both numbers of a roll (or all four numbers of a double). If you can't, you play just one number. If either number can be played but not both, you play the larger one. If you can't play either number, you lose your turn. If you roll doubles, you play as many numbers as you can.

Hitting and entering

A point occupied by a single checker of either colour is called a 'blot'. If an opposing checker lands on a blot, the blot is hit and the checker placed on the bar.

If you have one or more checkers on the bar, you must enter those checker(s) into the opposing home board. You enter a checker by moving it to an open point matching one of the numbers on the rolled dice. For example, if you roll 2 and 4, you can enter a checker onto either the opponent's two point or four point, so long as the point isn't occupied by two or more of your opponent's checkers.

If neither of the points are open, you lose your turn. If you can enter some but not all of your checkers, you have to enter as many as you can and then lose the rest of your turn.

After you've entered the last of your checkers, you have to play any unused numbers on the dice by moving the checker you entered or a different one.

Bearing off

Once you've moved all of your 15 checkers into your home board, you can start 'bearing off'. You do this by rolling a number that matches the point where the checker sits, and then removing that checker from the board. If there isn't a checker on the point shown by the roll, you have to make an ordinary move using a checker on a higher-numbered point. If you don't have any checkers on higher-numbered points, you must remove a checker from the highest point on which one of your checkers sits. You don't have to bear off if you can make an ordinary move.

The first player to bear off all 15 checkers wins the game.

Draughts

A board game of tactics where the aim is to capture your opponent's pieces by jumping over them, or prevent them from moving by blocking them in. The board is divided into 64 black and white squares and each player has 12 draughts.

How to play

Place the board so that the near right-hand corner square is white for both players. (A single corner is one from which a piece can only move in one direction; a double corner is one from which a piece can move into either of two squares.) Toss a coin to decide who has black or white. You and your opponent then place your draughts on the black squares, occupying the back three rows on the board and leaving the middle two rows clear. The white squares are not used in the game as the draughts move diagonally and so stay on the black squares.

Black makes the first move and then it's the other player's turn, and the game continues in this way. You can only move your draught one square at a time, in a diagonal to the left or right. You can jump over as many of your opponent's draughts as you like, as long as you are able. This is called 'taking' and the pieces are removed from the board.

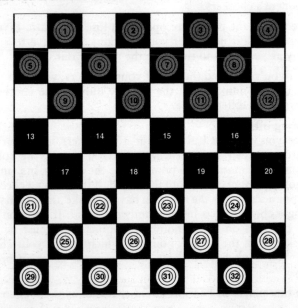

figure 27 the set up for draughts

If you don't take one or more draughts when you can do so, your opponent can take the draught with which the capture would have been made, force you to take the piece, or ignore the mistake. If your opponent chooses the first option, it's called 'huffing'. It doesn't count as a move but is carried out before the player makes his or her move.

Once you've moved your draught and taken your finger off it, you can't move it again on that turn. When you've infiltrated into enemy territory and reached your opponent's back row, your draught becomes a King and is crowned with a draught piece of the same colour not in play. Kings are very powerful as they can move backwards and forwards. A single layer draught piece can only move forwards.

If you play so skilfully that the opponent's draughts can't move, you win the game.

Tactics when starting

If you begin by playing to the sides, you need to block in your opponent and stop him getting any pieces crowned, because as soon as your opponent gets even one king, he may pursue you and break down all your potential side supports.

Playing to attack your opponent's double corner is a good game, but aim to get your draughts on squares 14–19. However, take care not to leave your pieces in such a position that your opponent can take more men than you can.

Standard opening moves

There are quite a few of these. It's worth learning one or two if you want to stay ahead of the game. See figure 27.

The Alma. Black moves 11 to 15, white 23 to 19, and then 8 to 11, 22 to 17 and 3 to 8.

The Ayrshire Lassie. This starts 11 to 15, 24 to 20, 8 to 11.

The Old Fourteenth. The start is 11 to 15, 23 to 19, 8 to 11, 22 to 17, 4 to 8.

Other winning tips

It's important to bear in mind right from the start of the game the position you're aiming for in the final stages, so all your moves should be made with this in mind. To have the last move you need to have your pieces in such a position that eventually you can block your opponent either by hemming them in to one side or by trapping their men in the centre. But if you can only do this by getting yourself blocked it's not worth it and may lose you the game. Having the last move in mind means you can often force your opponent to make certain moves which are helpful to you, instead of benefiting himself.

Chess

A game of strategy and tactics, chess is played by two opponents who move a set number of chessmen around the board, with the aim of cornering the other player's King so it can't escape. This situation is called 'Checkmate' and signifies the end of the game.

The 32 chessmen are divided into black and white pieces and each player starts the game with a King and Queen, two Rooks (also known as Castles), two Knights, two Bishops and eight Pawns (see figure 28).

figure 28 traditional chess pieces

Setting up your chessboard

Place the pieces on the chessboard following figure 29, with white pieces at the bottom and black at the top. You and your opponent should both be able to see a white square in the right-hand corner.

How the pieces move

To play chess, you need to learn the moves of the six pieces:

The Pawn can only move forward to an empty square directly in front of it. However, on its first move, it has the option of moving two squares. A pawn can also move diagonally to capture a piece in front on the left or in front on the right.

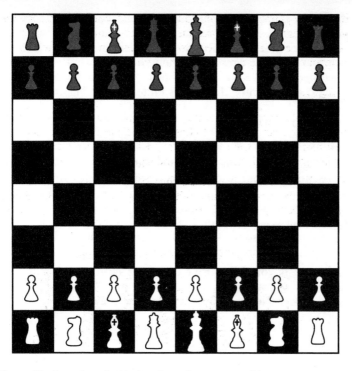

figure 29 chess board with the pieces in set-up position

Capturing moves are obligatory and the Pawn can't move diagonally to an empty square.

The Knight can jump over all the other chessmen, and is the only piece allowed to do this. It can move three squares either by moving one square forward or back, and two squares right or left; or by moving one square to the right or left, and two squares forward or back.

The Rook, after the Queen, has the most power on the board. It can move any number of squares up, down or sideways, but can only go in one direction at a time. It can't jump over any pieces. When it captures an opponent, it moves into that square.

The Bishop can move any number of squares but only diagonally. It can't leap over any pieces.

The Queen is the most powerful piece on the board. It can move any number of squares in any direction only if nothing is in its way. It can't jump over other pieces.

The King is the most important piece in the game, as its fate determines the outcome of the game. It can move one square in any direction. It can't leap over other pieces or move to a square where it could be captured. When you make a move that puts the other player's King at risk of being captured, you have to say 'Check' as a warning the King is under attack. The other player then has to make a move to protect the King. If this isn't possible, you win the game.

Special rules

Castling is where you can move your King and Rook in the same move. Its purpose is to keep the King safe. You can only do this **once** in any game, and only if there aren't any pieces between your King and Rook, if your King isn't under attack, and neither your King nor your Rook has moved yet. The King must move two squares towards the Rook, and the Rook must move to the square next to the King (on the other side).

Stalemate If your King isn't under attack, but you still can't move any of your pieces, then you call out 'Stalemate!' and the game is over. Neither player wins – it's a draw.

Gardening projects

Encouraging your children to develop an interest in gardening has so many benefits. It gets them outside in the fresh air, keeps them active and is a terrific way to get them interested in a new hobby.

Ways to involve the children

- Give children their own plot in the garden, where they can plant seeds of easy-to-grow flowers such as sunflowers, marigolds, zinnias and cosmos.
- Help them to grow vegetables in a pot – easy choices include tomatoes, carrots and radishes. This is also a cunning way to get them to eat more veg – they won't be able to resist sampling their own-grown vegetables.
- Encourage them to make their own themed garden. Themes can be based on fairy tales, games, interests and so on. Include plants and accessories that fit the theme. For instance an animal garden could include plants with animal names such as lamb's ear, catmint, toad lily, foxglove, snap dragon and bear's breeches. A seaside garden could include shells and

pebbles, sand and a mirror laid flat to suggest the sea. Your children are bound to come up with lots of other ideas once you've captured their interest.

- Help them develop an interest in wildlife. The best way of helping wildlife directly in your garden is to create specific habitats for the animals and insects you want to attract. Discuss with your children what they might need: a safe haven, food and water. Help them make nesting boxes for birds and bats; bird feeders; bird tables; ponds for frogs, newts and insects; compost heaps for worms; plant flowers for bees, butterflies and other insects; plant shrubs and trees. Trees also help trap unwanted gases like carbon dioxide that affect global warming – a useful lesson in how our actions affect the well-being of our planet.
- Some children might like to keep a wildlife diary, recording what they've seen in the garden every day.

Safety note

Avoid using any insecticides as these are very harmful to wildlife.

Bird feeder

You will need:

- clean plastic bottle or milk carton
- garden twine or string
- mesh or netting (e.g. the mesh bags that fruit comes in)
- scissors
- parcel tape
- peanuts or wild bird seed.

Safety note

Check that the peanuts you buy are safe for birds. The packet should have a label on it saying 'Safe Peanuts', which means that the levels of aflatoxins have been checked. Unchecked peanuts can kill birds.

Peanuts should only be given to birds between autumn and early spring, as after this time there will be young birds around who can't eat whole peanuts. Wild bird food can be kept until later in spring.

To make

Wash out the bottle and leave it to dry. Cut the bottom off the bottle. Place a piece of netting over the open end of the bottle. Fix it firmly in place with parcel tape. Tie string around the neck of the bottle. Fill the feeder with peanuts or wild bird seed.

Hang the feeder outside and wait for the birds to come and visit.

How to make an easy bird table

Attract birds to your garden with this simple bird table. Nail a piece of plywood (approximately 30 × 40 centimetres/12 × 16 inches) to the top of a fence post (about 1.5 metres/5 feet long). Nail four wooden batons (2 centimetres/1 inch deep) around the edge of the table, leaving a gap in each corner for rainwater to drain away and to stop the food being blown off. Fix the post into the ground. Place your table close to trees and shrubs to give birds cover, but make sure cats can't jump on it.

Food you can put out for the birds include peanuts (unsalted), fat (suet, dripping, meat fat, bacon rind), cheese, stale cakes, biscuits, pastry, dried fruits, apple, wild bird seed mixtures and sunflower seeds. Scatter rough seed mixes, sultanas, mealworms and fruit on the ground to attract birds such as blackbirds and thrushes. Keep the table clean and remove unwanted food to prevent diseases such as salmonella. Birds will appreciate a bowl of drinking water on the table, plus a shallow container filled with an inch or so of water on the ground to bathe in.

The birds will love this...

Make your own high-energy bird food, packed full of goodness to keep them going through the long winter months or when food is scarce. Melt or soften some lard or dripping, and mix in seeds, cake crumbs, oats, grated cheese and other goodies. Here are some different ways you can make it available to the birds in your garden:

- Press it between the scales of a fir cone. Fix a hanging wire or string to the cone and hang from a tree.
- Press the splodgy mixture to the bark of a tree.
- Attach a hanging loop through the base of an empty plastic yoghurt pot and pack it with the food. Hang the pot upside down from a branch in the garden.

Butterfly haven

Plant nectar-rich plants to attract butterflies or moths. To attract moths, plant white flowers and ones that open at night. A nettle patch tucked away in the corner of the garden provides food for certain caterpillar species of butterflies such as the Small Tortoiseshell and Peacock. Cut the patch back by half in mid-summer to encourage the growth of new shoots for the mid-summer brood of caterpillars.

Butterfly friendly plants for summer

Plant the following to bring butterflies into your garden: sedum, honesty, sweet rocket, honeysuckle, aster, candytuft, michaelmas daisy, nicotiana, arabis, dwarf phlox, yellow and annual alyssum, rosemary, hyssop, lavender, bergamot, thyme, wild and common marjoram, agrimony, thistles. Go for the old-fashioned, open, single-type flowers which the butterflies can get their proboscis into rather than the fancy double varieties. Keep a record of what butterflies you spot.

09

making things

In this chapter you will learn:
- how to teach your child to knit
- different painting techniques
- how to model and sculpt using different mediums
- how to make simple musical instruments.

From hand puppets to papier-mâché, printing to musical instruments, you and your children can make all sorts of things from objects found around the home. All the projects here are very easy, although you will need to supervise if craft knives or glue guns are involved.

Craft box

When it comes to making things, you never know what might come in handy, so keep anything and everything you think might be useful for creative projects. It's also a good way to recycle materials, so your children will be doing their bit for the planet, as well as exercising their artistic skills!

Here are some things that would be useful in a craft box:

- recycled materials, for example: boxes of all sizes, empty egg boxes, cereal packets, shoe boxes, picture postcards, fabric scraps and remnants, newspapers and magazines, empty matchboxes
- beads, sequins, buttons, yarn, ribbon, string
- good quality, wide masking tape
- balsa wood and dowel
- glitter
- cellophane
- adhesive – different types of strength
- paper – all sorts, for example: wrapping paper, cellophane, packaging, gold and silver
- cardboard, thin and thick
- old photos
- scissors, craft knife
- paints – poster, acrylic, household
- colouring pencils, felt-tips, permanent markers.

Alternatively you can buy materials for your children's projects from craft shops, although this can get quite expensive, so be selective. Useful items you can buy online or in person include pipe cleaners, dolls' hair and self-adhesive eyes.

A word about paper, as this is the staple element of practically every creative project, it's important to choose the right type to suit what you're doing:

Construction paper or sugar paper – coarse paper which comes in different colours and weights. Good for drawing, watercolour, crayon, charcoal, making cut-outs and greetings cards.

Cartridge paper – good for all types of drawing and painting and printing projects.

Card – comes in a variety of weights, sizes and colours. You can also get corrugated card. Good for making puppets etc.

Paints are equally important. Poster paint is widely used in craft projects for children, but it isn't waterproof. Acrylic is a more practical choice if you want a long-lasting waterproof paint which you don't need to varnish, unless you want a special effect.

Pop-up card

This is a beautifully simple pop-up card that can be turned into any type of greetings card. Draw any type of bird you like – a fluffy Easter chick would be perfect for an Easter card.

You will need:

- 2 sheets of paper
- glue stick
- scissors
- felt-tips.

Take a sheet of A4 paper and fold it in half. Find the middle of the crease and cut a horizontal line 5 centimetres (2 inches) from the edge of the fold inwards. Turn the paper sideways and fold back each flap of paper in turn to make two triangles. Open out the card carefully. Turn the card sideways and, gripping the cut edge of each triangle with your thumb and forefinger, pull them up and apart from each other. At the same time pinch together the tops of the triangles and fold flat towards you. Close the card and there will be a V-shaped chunk cut out of it. Press down on the folds and open the card again. A bird's beak will open and shut. Glue another sheet of paper to the card to hide the cut-out, taking care to avoid the beak. Let it dry. Draw a circle around the beak and draw on two beady eyes. Paint and leave to dry or use felt-tips to perfect your design.

You can easily adapt this card by making a horizontal cut in the card lower down, halfway between the centre and the bottom of the card. This time, you just have one triangle to pinch together along the centre fold, so you end up with a triangle lying flat on the paper. Close the card and there will be a chunk out of the card in the shape of a '7'. Press the fold down and open the card to reveal a pop-up that you can turn into a vase. Draw some flowers in the vase, or cut out flower shapes, and you have the perfect card for Mother's Day.

How to knit

Knitting is one of those crafts that once learned is never forgotten. Show your children how to knit and you'll be passing on a skill they can draw on at any time. And if anyone in your family has the temerity to suggest that knitting is just for women, remind that men have knitted throughout history!

Casting on

Make a slipknot with the yarn around one knitting needle (figure 30a). Hold the needle in your right hand and the short end of the wool around your right little finger. Hold the wool in your left hand and slip it around your thumb (figure 30b). Put the needle into the loop from below and slide the loop formed on to the needle (Figure 30c). Don't pull the loop too tight (figure 30d). Cast on like this until you have the right number of stitches.

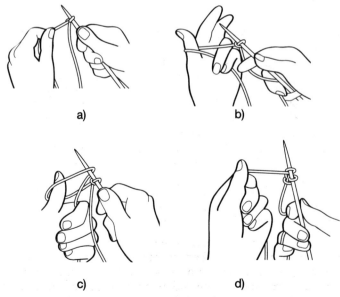

a)   b)

c)   d)

figure 30 casting on

Plain knitting

Take the needle holding the stitches in your left hand and the empty needle in your right. Place the right needle into the first stitch, and under the left needle (see figure 31a).

Starting with the wool on the right of the needle, take it around the point, and back over it from left to right (figure 31b).

Draw the right needle and wool towards you carefully to form a new stitch on the right needle (figure 31c) and slide the old loop off the left needle (figure 31d). Continue to the end of the row.

Turn the work around so that the needle holding the stitches is again in your left hand and you are ready to start the next row.

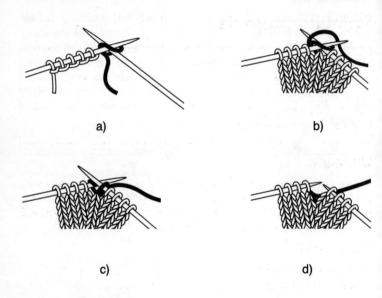

a)

b)

c)

d)

figure 31 plain knitting

Casting off

Knit two stitches on the right needle. Take the right, or first stitch, over the left or second stitch and slide it off the needle to the left. Knit one more stitch on to the right needle and repeat, taking the right over the left again. Continue until you have one stitch left. Break off the wool and bring the end up through the last loop. Pull tight.

Knitting a scarf

Here's a very easy pattern for a scarf knitted in plain stitch. The wool you use determines the size of knitting needles you use – the finer the wool, the thinner the knitting needles. Bigger needles and thicker wool will knit up more quickly.

You will need:

- 1 ball of Chunky yarn (Bulky weight in US)
- 1 pair of 7 mm knitting needles.

Cast on 37 stitches. Knit in plain stitch (also called garter stitch) until your scarf measures about 1 metre or as long as you want it to be. Cast off.

Painting projects

A quick guide to mixing colours

Red and blue = purple
Red and green = brown
Blue and yellow = green
Red and yellow = orange

Marbling

This technique has been used for hundreds of years and can be used to create some beautiful patterns which you can turn into wrapping paper or frame as a picture. Experiment with different colour combinations and types of paper.

You will need:

- sheets of newspaper
- foil roasting tray
- large jug of cold water
- marble paint in different colours from craft shop
- paper or card, cut to fit tray
- pencil.

Cover the table with sheets of newspaper to protect it. Fill the tray with about 2 centimetres (1 inch) water. Gradually add a few drops of paint. Choose a main colour and then add smaller drops of other colours. Swirl the paints around with a sharpened pencil so you get an interesting pattern with all the colours slightly merging. Gently pull the paper over the surface of the water and leave it there to soak up the paint. However, make sure it doesn't get submerged by the water. Taking one end of the paper, carefully slide it back from the surface. As you pull, the paint will transfer from the tray to the paper, leaving you with a stunning pattern. Leave to dry flat on newspaper.

Marble painting

You will need:

- circle of paper (cut to fit base of bowl)
- marbles
- poster paints, diluted with water
- small containers
- round washing-up bowl
- plastic spoons.

Put the paper in the bottom of the bowl. Fill the containers with different coloured paints. Drop a marble into a paint container and then lift it out with the spoon. Drop it onto the paper in the bowl. Tip the bowl backwards, forwards and sideways so the marble rolls all over the paper, leaving paint marks. When the marble has transferred all of its paint to the paper, dip it again in the same or different coloured paint. Carry on like this until you have a pattern of marble paint trails all over the paper. Take the paper out and leave to dry.

Printing with paints

Sponge painting is a less messy, easier version of potato printing, where you cut out a pattern in the sponge, apply paint and then press onto paper. You can achieve some impressive results with this type of printing which can be used to make wrapping paper, posters, greetings cards or interesting pictures.

You will need:

- small non-stick sponges
- craft knife
- paintbrushes
- poster paints
- large sheets of white paper.

Peel off the scouring surface of the sponge. Using a craft knife, cut out a design in the sponge. Simple shapes work best, such as circles or flowers. Dip into paint and print away.

Paint blowing

This is a very simple way of painting, and great fun, but whatever you do don't suck!

You will need:

- paper
- straws
- liquid poster paints.

Dilute different coloured poster paints with water and put a couple of drops of the same colour onto the paper. Using the straw, blow the paint all over the paper. If you turn the paper around, it's easier to blow the paint in different directions. Repeat using other colours to create interesting effects. Using primary colours shows how well colours combine to make different ones.

Bubble painting

You will need:

- paper
- containers with wide tops (e.g. plastic cups, yoghurt pots)
- powder or liquid poster paints
- washing-up liquid
- straws.

Put a squirt of paint and a squirt of washing-up liquid into one of the containers. Add a little water and mix well until the mixture is thin enough to blow bubbles with. Using the straw, blow into the mixture until bubbles rise above the top. Rest a piece of paper on the bubbles, which will burst and leave a mark on the paper. You won't get a very dark pattern as the effect of the bubble bursting is quite light but it will still make an interesting effect and is lots of fun.

Leaf prints

You will need:

- interesting leaves, with well-defined shapes
- soft wax crayon
- white paper.

Place a leaf on a sheet of thin paper so the veins are facing upwards. Put a sheet of white paper over it and, keeping it in place, very gently rub the crayon over the surface of the paper. You should see an imprint of the veins on the paper.

Making a collage

A collage is a brilliant project to share with your kids as there aren't any set rules. It basically involves glueing a selection of items onto a board or paper, and it's entirely up to you what you have in your collage. It's a craft where you can let your imagination soar sky-high. A collage could revolve around a theme such as food, fashion, or travel; or make a statement, for example, why animals should not be killed for their fur; or be a photographic record of family events or a visual memory of an important date. Alternatively, it doesn't actually have to be anything, except a pleasing arrangement of items.

Collect what you need. These could include:

- magazines, brochures, newspapers
- wrapping paper
- family photos
- old receipts, invites, tickets
- felt-tip pens
- colouring pencils
- glitter
- glue stick, liquid adhesive
- paints and paintbrushes
- string, buttons, ribbon, beads, sequins
- cotton wool
- fabric and wool remnants
- miscellaneous household objects such as coins, stamps, takeaway leaflets, brochures, small empty cartons, bottle tops, tiny plastic toys, keys, sweet wrappers – basically anything you can find.

First, cover the area you're working on with a big sheet of paper or a plastic cloth. Then gather together everything you might want to use in your collage. If your children find it difficult to get started – and the thing about making a collage is that anything goes – get them to tear out images from magazines that appeal to them. Once you've assembled a pile of pictures, sift through the mass of stuff on the table and pick out things to go with the pictures. Some children might find this type of 'freefall' art a little scary, but keep encouraging them to use their imagination. When you have an idea of what you want in your collage, you can start arranging your picture on a posterboard or card. Once you're happy with the arrangement, glue everything in place. You may find you need stronger adhesive for some of the items in your collage.

Modelling projects

Papier-mâché

You will need:

- newspaper
- 2 large bowls
- wallpaper paste (this keeps longer than the traditional flour and water recipe)
- water.

Tear newspaper into strips. Dip each strip with paste. Hold the strip over the bowl and run it through your fingers to squeeze off excess paste. Stick the newspaper strip over the form you want to papier-mâché – balloons, plastic bottles, rolled up newspaper – and smooth it down with your fingers. Completely cover your creation with a layer of newspaper strips. They should all be overlapping. After one layer has been applied, let it dry for about 24 hours.

Add another layer of newspaper strips and let it dry for another 24 hours. Repeat this process until you get the desired effect, but you should have at least three layers. Finish with a layer of tissue paper for an extra smooth finish.

Quick alternative

Soak paper (egg boxes, coloured card and recycled paper) in a bucket of water overnight. Take handfuls of soggy paper and put them in a blender, adding plenty of water. Whizz to a pulp. Strain excess water. You can use this pulp to make shapes, for example, puppet heads or animals. Allow the shapes to dry and paint. If you're using poster paints, you can add a layer of varnish, although you don't need to do this with acrylic paints.

Play dough

Easier to use with younger children than Plasticine, play dough is a wonderful, squidgy, elastic substance which can be made into all sorts of shapes. Roll it, flatten it, put it into moulds – the possibilities are endless.

Ingredients

4 cups of plain flour
1 cup of salt
1–2 cups of hot water (from the tap)
2 tsp of vegetable oil.

To make your own, much cheaper version of Play-Doh, mix together two cups of flour, one cup of salt and one cup of water. Add one tablespoon of vegetable oil. Add food colouring to water then slowly add the liquid to the mixture until it's the right consistency. Knead until smooth. Stored in a plastic bag in an airtight container, the play dough should last about a week.

This salt dough is also great for making Christmas decorations, little gifts or more ambitious sculptures. Store the dough in an airtight container in the fridge and it should last a while.

Mix the salt and flour together, and add the water. Work in with your hands until the dough is elastic, then add the vegetable oil. If the mixture is too sticky, add more flour; if it's too dry, add more water. Knead the dough until it's smooth and elastic. It's now ready to use. To add interest you could add glitter or food colouring to the dough. The dough can be moulded in any shape you like before being baked in the oven at 200°C/400°F – the exact cooking time depends on the size of your sculpture. Once it has cooled, you can paint it with poster or acrylic paints. Make sure you paint and varnish everything made with salt dough, and keep them in a cool, dry place.

Soap carving

This is a great way to introduce your children to sculpture as soap is such a satisfying medium to work with. It's soft and malleable and you can make all sorts of animals and objects with it. All you need are bars of white soap (buy the cheapest) and a sharpened lolly stick to carve it with. Potato peelers are excellent for shaving off pieces of soap. Using pictures for reference, carve the soap into the shape you want. Keep turning the soap over as you work so you get a three-dimensional look.

Making musical instruments

Paper and comb

This is one of the easiest and best known home-made instruments which makes a surprisingly effective sound.

You will need:

• small comb
• sheet of tissue paper.

To make

Fold a small piece of tissue paper over the comb, hold up to your mouth, and blow through it. Move your mouth along the comb to achieve different sounds.

Thimble and jar lid

You might not think so, but with just a thimble and a jar lid you can get an impressive rhythm going that you can use to accompany friends playing other instruments.

You will need:

- a jar lid – for example, a jam jar
- two thimbles.

To make

Put a thimble on the first and second fingers of your right hand and tap the jar lid. You can change the tone by using the fingers on your left hand. The fewer fingers you use to tap the jar lid, the more intense and prolonged the tones. With practice you can make simple tunes by quickly raising and lowering your fingers to make different notes.

Maracca

You will need:

- empty fruit juice carton with screw top
- stick (30 centimetres/12 inches long)
- rice grains
- glue.

To make

Make a small hole in the top and bottom of the carton. Push the stick right through both holes so you have the same length of stick either end of the carton. Drop a few rice grains in through the screw top opening. Put a little glue on this and screw on the top. Keep the stick stable by gluing around the two holes it passes through. (A washed margarine tub with the lid firmly Sellotaped on would work equally as well.)

Bean rattle

This home-made bean rattle makes a noise just like the maracas used in Cuban and Mexican popular music.

You will need:

- cardboard tube (mailing or kitchen towel tube)
- glue
- string
- beans, rice or gravel
- acrylic paints.

To make

Cut two circles of thin card, both about two inches larger in diameter than the tube. Put glue on the back of one of the circles and place it over one end of the tube, pulling down the edges and pleating them to ensure they stick neatly to the tube. Wind string around the card two or three times, tie and glue into place. Now fill the tube with beans, rice or gravel (to about half full) and secure the other end in the same way. Decorate your rattle with beautiful designs using acryllic paints.

Rubber band banjo

Very easy to make, you'll be surprised how like an actual banjo this sounds.

You will need:

- cardboard box, 12 × 10 × 5 centimetres (5 × 4 × 2 inches)
- four rubber bands in different sizes.

To make

Using the point of a knife, cut a semi-circular sound hole and a slot in the top of the box. From a piece of heavy cardboard cut a bridge shape as shown in figure 32. The bottom part of the bridge should fit tightly in the slot cut in the top of the box.

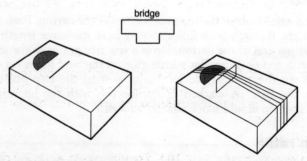

figure 32 rubber band banjo

Stretch the rubber bands around the box, passing them over the bridge. As they're different sizes, each rubber band will make a different noise, the smaller ones being stretched more tightly than the larger ones. This finishes your banjo, which you play by plucking the strings with a finger or a toothpick.

Tambourine

This is made from the top of a round cardboard box, or round margarine lid, with small bells fastened to it. You can buy the bells from craft shops or remove them from old toys.

You will need:

- the lid of a round cardboard box/margarine lid
- bell hooks
- six small bells
- safety pins.

To make

Cut slits in the side of the box or lid. Put the bell hooks through the slits and fasten them in place with safety pins. Attach bells. To play, set up a rhythm by shaking and striking it against your knee or with your fist.

Earthenware drum

You will need:

- clay flowerpot
- heavy paper.

To make

Stretch a wet sheet of heavy paper tightly across the top of the large clay flowerpot. Secure with strong cord. As the paper dries, it shrinks and makes an excellent drumhead.

Sand block

Rub together these sands blocks and you'll get that shuffling effect used in a lot of dance music. Sandpaper comes in different textures from smooth to coarse, so the texture you choose will affect the sound.

You will need:

- two wooden blocks, $12 \times 10 \times 5$ centimetres ($5 \times 4 \times 2$ inches)
- one sheet sandpaper.

To make

Cut sandpaper to fit wooden blocks and then glue to one side. Leave to dry and you have an instant instrument!

Pin piano

Believe it or not, you can actually play tunes on a pin piano as it contains a full octave of notes, enabling you to play a wide variety of tunes including Home Sweet Home and Auld Lang Syne. You play the pin piano with a nail, which is tapped against the pins.

You will need:

- a piece of soft wood, 35 × 8 centimetres (14 × 3 inches)
- a pencil
- eight panel pins – the longest you can find.

To make

Using a pencil, draw a line along the centre of the wood. Make eight dots on the line, evenly spaced, about 3 centimetres apart. Hammer a pin into the first dot. Each subsequent pin needs to be hammered in more deeply than the one before. This gives each pin a different tone so it can become a note in the scale. The deeper you drive a pin in, the higher the pitch of its tone.

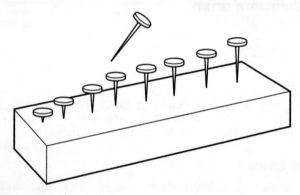

figure 33 pin piano

Musical bottles

By filling juice bottles with different amounts of water, you can create some catchy tunes. Take six glass juice bottles or very tall drinking glasses and fill them with different heights of water to make a six note scale. (Use your voice or a piano to help you do this.) Number your bottles one to six, the first bottle holding the most water.

Here's a guide to get you started, using Snapple bottles.

1st bottle	2nd bottle	3rd bottle	4th bottle	5th bottle	6th bottle
5½in water	4in water	3¼in water	3in water	2¼in water	2in water

To play these tunes, tap the bottles near the rim with a small spoon or stick.

Jingle Bells

333 333 35123
444 4433 3355421

Twinkle Twinkle Little Star

11 55 66 5 44 33 22 1
55 44 33 2 55 44 33 2
11 55 66 5 44 33 22 1

This Old Man

535 535 6543234
345 1 111 12345

5224321

Try composing your own songs. Add two more juice bottles to your collection and you'll be able to make a whole octave!

10

children's parties

In this chapter you will learn:
- tips for a stress-free party
- games to let off steam
- games to calm noisy children.
- how to organize a treasure hunt.

Children's birthday parties have become very elaborate and expensive affairs these days, so no wonder parents find them so stressful. Chances are your child will be obliged to invite the whole class, which means you could have up to 20 children rampaging through your house, and then there's the headache of how to keep them entertained. Parties can also cost you a small fortune, if you factor in the cost of hiring an entertainer, laying on a spread, and those dreaded, but expected, party bags.

The ideas that follow don't cost a lot and will keep children happy and occupied. It is also important to be organized and to keep the party food simple.

Tips for a stress-free party

- Plan your child's party like a military operation so the children don't get the chance to misbehave. If you're worried about your house being messed up or haven't a lot of room, hold the party in a church hall or similar venue.

- Make a list of all the games and activities they're going to play, in the order they're going to play them.

- Begin with games which help everyone feel included. There might be children at the party who don't know many people or feel too shy to join in, so choose games that are easy to play and don't make anyone feel silly or left out.

- Once tea is over, children will have a renewed burst of energy, but obviously it's not a good idea to have them careering around after they've just eaten, so choose sitting-down games, like pass the parcel.

- Enlist the help of other parents. While parents may see parties as a way of offloading their kids and sloping off for some 'me' time, there's no reason why they shouldn't give you a hand. If you feel extra hospitable, lure them in with a glass of wine (or soft drink if they're driving) and hot food. (Parents can often be as hungry as their children, and if they've come a long way they will welcome the offer of a bite to eat.)

- Make sure parents and children are clear about the start and finish time.

Games to start with

Who am I?

This is a great ice-breaker if you have a large group of children who don't know each other.

You will need:

- some small sticky notes (Post-its)
- a pen.

How to play

Write the name of a famous person or character on a sticky note for each party-goer. Characters can be dead or alive, real or imaginary. Making sure that the player can't see it, stick the note to their forehead. If you prefer you can pin a larger piece of paper on each player's back rather than use sticky notes. This may be better on a hot day or when the children can't be trusted to keep their sticky note on their forehead! When everyone is named, there will be a lot of giggling at first. Then the players mix and walk around the room asking the sort of questions that can be answered by 'Yes', 'No' and 'Maybe' to try to work out who they are.

For example, a child with the character of Cinderella might ask the following questions and receive the following answers:

Q Am I a girl?
A Yes

Q Am I alive?
A No

Q Am I in history books?
A No

Q Am I old?
A No

Q Am I famous?
A Yes.

Q Am I real?
A No

Q Am I a film character?
A Yes

Q Am I in story books?
A Yes

Q Am I rich?
A No

Q Am I nice?
A Yes

Q Am I beautiful?
A Yes

and so on...

Tip

Choose your names carefully so that all the party-goers will know the characters and be able to answer the questions. You can also use ordinary people, such as the children's teacher or even the name of the party child. Be prepared to help the children out with hints if necessary.

Variations

Use famous 'couples' (such as Prince Charming and Cinderella, Batman and Robin). People not only have to guess their own identity but find their partner. You will need a much bigger number of players for this to work, as it becomes too easy to look at other people's names and just ask straight out if you are their opposite number.

Feather

You will need:

- feather
- tablecloth or piece of sheeting – preferably round, although this is not essential
- music player.

How to play

Sit the children cross-legged on the floor and ask them to hold on to the edge of the tablecloth and stretch it between themselves until it is tight. Drop the feather into the centre.

When you start the music, the children begin to tip the tablecloth (although they must remain sitting at all times) and blow frantically to keep the feather away from them. When you stop the music, whoever the feather is nearest to gets a penalty letter (for instance DUCK, as a duck could have produced the feather, but you can use PIG or DONKEY or whatever you wish, depending on how long you want the game to continue). If the feather touches a child at any time, even when the music is playing, they also get a letter. The game ends when one child completes the word.

Playing this way – with no apparent winners and no real loser – is popular with children, who tend to laugh when one of their friends gets another letter.

The chocolate game

You will need:

- a wrapped bar of chocolate
- a plate
- a knife and fork
- some dressing-up items (at least a hat, scarf and gloves)
- 2 dice.

How to play

A fast and frantic game involving eating chocolate, so it should be pretty popular! Everyone sits in a circle with a bar of chocolate on a plate in the middle. Have knives and forks next to it, and assorted dressing-up clothes – hat, scarf, gloves etc. You take it in turns to roll the dice on the floor, passing them round to your left. If you throw a double six, you rush to put on the dressing up clothes, and then try to cut the chocolate bar with the knife and fork and eat some of it. Meanwhile the other players carry on throwing the dice in turn. When someone throws a double six you have to take off the clothes and hand them to that player who then has to put the clothes on and try to cut the chocolate. Continue until the chocolate is all gone.

The straw game

You will need:

- a bowl per player, plus 2 extra
- a plastic straw for each player and a few spare
- small sweets (candy).

How to play

Divide the children into two teams. Place the bowls in two lines opposite each other (either along the length of a table or on the ground), with a straw next to each bowl. In the first bowl in each line place 15–20 small sweets. (Avoid any with nuts in them unless you are absolutely sure that none of the children at the party has a nut allergy.)

The children each stand or kneel by a bowl. There will be one spare bowl at the end of the line. At your signal the first player begins to transfer the sweets, one by one, from their bowl to the next bowl along, using only their straw. Absolutely no hands are allowed, even if a sweet is dropped! The next player begins to transfer the sweets as soon as they arrive in his or her bowl into the next one, and so on down the line until all the sweets arrive in the final bowl, at which point that team is declared the winner.

Variation

This version works with unequal numbers of children and requires less props and less space – and takes more time. It's fun for a mixed age group of children, in which case try to distribute the children fairly and make sure that the older children encourage the younger ones, who will be quite a lot slower at the game. Have two bowls per team.

One player starts by transferring the sweets from one bowl to the next. When all the sweets are transferred, the next player comes up and transfers them back and so on, until the last player has transferred all the sweets. If you have uneven teams, one player can go twice.

Pin the tail on the donkey

You will need:

- scarf as blindfold
- large drawing of donkey pinned onto a board
- separate tail of donkey made out of thick card or wool
- Blu-Tack or sticky tape to pin the tail on donkey (safer than the traditional drawing pins)
- small prize.

How to play

Each player takes it in turn while blindfolded to pin the tail on the donkey. Each attempt is marked on the board, and the person who is closest to pinning the tail in the right place wins. To make it more difficult you can always spin the children round three times to disorientate them and then guide them to the board to pin the tail.

Musical bumps

You will need:

- CD player with dancing music or children's favourites
- small prizes.

How to play

The children dance around in the centre of the room until the music stops, when they must sit down on the floor as quickly as possible. The last one down is 'out'. It can often work better to award a prize to the last two or three children standing rather than try to pick one winner.

Musical statues

How to play

Everyone starts dancing to the music, but must freeze the minute the music stops. Anyone unable to keep perfectly still is 'out'. The winner is the last person to be out.

Musical chairs

You will need:

- CD player or similar with dancing music or children's favourites
- chair or cushion for each player (improvise by cutting squares or circles out of an old plastic tablecloth or sheet)
- some small prizes.

How to play

Arrange the chairs or cushions around the room, leaving space for the children to skip around and dance. Two lines of chairs in the centre of the room works well, as does a ring around the edges. Alternatively, scatter cushions around the area randomly.

The children dance and skip around while the music plays. When the music stops they must race to sit on a chair or cushion. In the first round there will a space for everybody, but then you remove one chair after each round and the child who doesn't find somewhere to sit is eliminated. Supervise carefully as children can get carried away in this game.

Musical numbers

You will need:

- large sheet of paper, old sheeting or a plastic tablecloth
- scissors
- marker pen
- small prizes.

Cut a large circle of paper, old sheeting or old plastic tablecloth for every child at the party, and number each circle with large numbers. Also have prepared a few small prizes, one for each round you are going to play, wrapped up and marked with corresponding numbers. So, for example, if you have 20 children and hope to play five rounds, you would have 20 pieces of paper marked 1 to 20, and, say, five prizes marked 3, 7, 12, 15 and 19.

How to play

Scatter the paper circles around the room and get the children dancing as before. When the music stops the children must sit down on a piece of paper. Then announce the magic number for that round and see who has won the little prize!

Hot potato dressing

You will need:

- a large bag or basket with dressing-up clothes, old hats and scarves, odd socks and boots etc. If you can include some joke items such as fake ears and plastic spectacles the children will enjoy the game even more.

How to play

Form the children into a circle and give the bag to the birthday child. Put some cheerful music on. While the music plays, the children pass the bag around the circle. When the music stops, whoever is holding the bag must reach in and pull out one article of clothing (make sure they choose quickly without looking) and put it on.

If you have a lot of children, or younger children, you can have two bags circulating simultaneously (and they will be lighter for the children to manage).

Wobbling bunnies

How to play

All the players have to hop about the room pretending to be rabbits, holding their hands up next to their ears. Whenever you shout out 'Hunter' the bunnies have to stop moving and freeze until you call out 'Hunter's gone'. Anyone losing their balance or falling over is out.

Spider and flies

How to play

Choose one child to be the spider, the rest are flies. Tell the children that they are going to play tag, and that the spider is going to try to catch the flies. Every fly that the spider catches becomes part of its web, holding hands with the spider and trying to catch the remaining flies (which can take some co-ordination and concentration)! The last player to be caught becomes the new spider.

Scratch cat

How to play

Scratch cat walks around the room on all fours. The other players have to try to touch the cat on the head, back or legs. If Scratch Cat touches or tags any of them with his hands, that person becomes the new Scratch Cat. You can have more than one Scratch Cat if you wish.

Games to use up energy

Duck, duck, goose

This is another chasing game, the rules of which can be found on p. 132.

Blind man's buff

An energetic game with no prizes. However, you do need plenty of space to play this. You will also need a scarf to serve as a blindfold.

How to play

Blindfold one of the players (it's a good idea to choose one of the more confident children to begin with). Turn them around a couple of times to disorientate them and let them go to try to catch other players. Once they catch someone, they have two or three goes at guessing who it is. If they guess correctly, that person is then blindfolded. If not, they carry on playing until they correctly identify someone. (Watch this game carefully to avoid bumps into furniture and walls.)

Calming games

Sleeping lions

How to play

Everyone has to lie on the floor and keep completely still. Anyone who moves is out. The person who lies completely still the longest is the winner. Another child or an adult can try to distract the sleeping lions and get them to wake.

Tortoise race

A good game to quieten the mood.

How to play

All the players line up against a wall. On the word 'Go', they have to walk forward as slowly as possible to the far wall. The person who is the last to finish wins. Players are disqualified if they stop or change direction.

Pass the parcel

For this game you will need a small present wrapped in loads of layers of newspaper.

How to play

Everyone sits on the floor in a circle. When the music starts a parcel is passed from person to person. When the music stops, whoever holds the parcel at that moment is allowed to unwrap a layer. Once a layer has been unwrapped, the music starts again, and the parcel continues to be passed around. The game carries on in this way until someone unwraps the very last layer and wins the prize. A version of this game is to put a tiny present in between each layer, so every child gets something.

Hunt the thimble

You will need a thimble for this game, or a similarly small object.

How to play

Choose one child (usually the party child) to be the first to hide the thimble. All the other children leave the room. When the thimble is hidden, the children are called back in and race to be the first to find it. Whoever does so is the next to hide the thimble, and the game continues.

Before you start, gather all the children together and make sure that they understand the rules: the thimble must be hidden in such a way that it can be seen without moving furniture, opening drawers and cupboards, and otherwise disturbing your room! Give them an example of a good hiding place, and point out that by cleverly hiding the thimble against something of a similar colour or shape, it can be very hard to find.

Variations

Partnering up: This is a good game for sorting children into pairs for the next game. Hide two thimbles at once, and the children who find them become partners.

Mixed ages: If you're playing with children and adults of mixed ages, try hiding two different objects of different sizes: a tiny button for the adults, and a thimble for the children.

A treasure hunt

All children love a treasure hunt and it's a really good way to end a party. However, allow yourself time to prepare it before the party starts. Collect a large number of little treasures suitable for hiding around the house or garden, for example, sweets, games, small stuffed toys, cheap CDs, pen sets and so on. Scour your local shops and you're bound to find some very inexpensive gifts.

Hide the treasure carefully. Some should be very easy to see; some can be hidden more seriously. Don't forget to put some little things at eye level too. Any edible treasure should be easy to find so that it doesn't linger in the garden. Get older children to help you hide the treasure.

Gather the children together, give each child a loot bag and an indication of what sort of treasure they may find, and tell them where to start hunting. You may want to allocate an older child or adult to make sure that everyone finds an appropriate number of treasures.

Make sure you hide away any toys or sweets which are your family's own property. It can be very embarrassing asking for something back which the party guest proudly thinks is theirs because they found it.

Ending the party

It can be difficult ending a children's party and there's always at least one child who doesn't want to go. A good incentive is to give every guest a party bag as they leave. Look in discount stores or pound shops for inexpensive items to fill bags – such as balloons, games/puzzles, sweets, stickers, playing cards, dice, erasers, key rings, fridge magnets, marbles, jewellery, hair slides, badges, bubbles, bead kits and mini animals. Make sure all the parents know exactly when they should come and collect their child so you're not left looking after little Johnny into the early evening. Parents can also have a habit of lingering once they've arrived so you can end up with another party on your hands if you're not careful! You may not mind this of course, in which case it's worth getting in a bottle of wine, soft drinks and some light refreshments. You could also invite just your close friends to stay on with their children, so the atmosphere is a little calmer. Sit down and relax (after enlisting the aid of parents to help you clear up) and congratulate yourself on having survived another children's party!

taking it further

The internet is an excellent source of information for children's games, crafts and activities. It's impossible to list them all, but here is a selection of some of the best.

Activity Village: **www.activityvillage.co.uk**

Crammed with ideas to keep the kids amused indoors and out.

Kids Ark is a child-centred site which promotes traditional pursuits from conkers to pond-dipping. Access the site at **http://web.ukonline.co.uk/conker/**

Days out

www.enjoyengland.com

Information about outings and holidays in England.

www.usatourist.com

Independent guide to travel to the United States.

www.daysoutwiththekids.co.uk

Click on the map and find out what's on offer in your area.

www.allkids.co.uk

Even includes best picnic sites in UK

www.sustrans.org.uk

Charity promoting cycling for all where you can find out about cycling routes throughout the UK.

www.history.uk.com/brass_rubbing

Learn all about brass rubbing.

Museums

www.museums.co.uk

Guide to museums in your area.

www.exploratorium.edu

Superb interactive site that explores and explains science in everyday life.

Zoos and safari parks

www.aboutbritain.com

Details about animal attractions in Britain

www.britainsfinest.co.uk
www.safaripark.co.uk

Safari and wildlife park guide

Fossil hunting

www.discoveringfossils.co.uk
www.ukfossils.co.uk

Fossils and fossil collecting in the UK. Featuring hundreds of fossil yielding locations, geological guides, in a fossil hunters community

Parks

UK www.nationalpark.org.uk

USA www.nps.gov

Walking

www.ramblers.org.uk

Camping

UK www.camp-sites.co.uk

USA www.gocampingamerica.com

Brass rubbing

www.history.uk.com

Games

www.activityvillage.co.uk

A huge variety of children's games, indoor and out and for every type of occasion.

www.gameskidsplay.net

An excellent resource for all those games you remember from your childhood.

www.family-reunion.com

Ideas for family gatherings.

Children's Party Games (Collins Gem), HarperCollins

The Best Party Games by Joseph Edmundson (Pan Originals). Out of print but you can buy it secondhand from www.amazon.com

Card games

www.pagat.com

Excellent site with rules and instructions for every card and board game you can possibly think of.

www.fun.familyeducation.com
www.thehouseofcards.com

Board games

www.mastersgames.com

Rules for every sort of board game, which you can also buy.

www.back-gammon.co.uk

Clear instructions for backgammon beginners with useful photographs

Chess for beginners:

http://chess.about.com/od/beginners
www.chessdryad.com
www.geocities.com/CapeCanaveral/Lab/835

Crafts and interests

www.enchantedlearning.com

Knitting

www.bhkc.co.uk
www.nationalknittingweek.co.uk

Homemade musical instruments

www.traditionalmusic.co.uk/its-easy-to-make-music/make-music-0009.htm

Great ideas for homemade instruments.

Textile designs

www.polo-shirts.co.uk

Sell cheap plain T-shirts and sweatshirts, plus Berol pens and paint, The site also carries useful tips and techniques for textile projects including tie-dyeing and fabric painting.

Juggling

www.pandas.currantbun.com/Juggling/Jugg.html

Card tricks

www.card-trick.com

www.howtodotricks.com

Gardening for children

www.bbc.co.uk/gardening
www.thekidsgarden.co.uk
www.wildlife-gardening.co.uk; www.overthegardengate.net

Ideas for attracting wildlife to your garden

Garden birds

www.rspb.org.uk
www.bbc.co.uk/nature/animals